COPYRIGHT © 2020 DAVID L VARNER
All rights reserved.

No part of this publication may be reproduced, stored in a retrieval system, or transmitted in any form or by any means, electronic, mechanical, photocopying, recording, scanning or otherwise, except as permitted under Section 107 or 108 of the 1976 United States Copyright Act with the prior written permission of the author.

THE SALES CHECKLIST™
*Get it right every time*

www.thesaleschecklist.info

ISBN   979-8-62-420032-6

# THE
# SALES
# CHECKLIST™

• • •

## Get it right every time!

by
**David L. Varner**

# TABLE OF CONTENTS

| | |
|---|---:|
| Introduction | ix |
| The Sales Checklist™ — Get It Right Every Time! | 1 |
| Making the Connection between Selling and Checklists | 7 |
| Where It All Begins | 13 |
| Identifying the Problem | 15 |
| Reality Sets In | 35 |
| The Sales Checklist™ | 45 |
|     1) Customer Fit | 51 |
|     2) Trigger Event | 65 |
|     3) Sales Target | 77 |
|     4) Decision-Making Process | 83 |
|     5) Decision Influencers | 88 |
|     6) Mentor | 97 |
|     7) Trigger Priority | 103 |
|     8) Alternatives | 109 |
|     9) Our Solution Ranking | 114 |
|     10) Individual Impact | 118 |
| Epilogue | 123 |

*To my wife and girlfriend, Chris*

# INTRODUCTION

WHAT IS IN THIS BOOK WILL SEEM ALMOST RIDICULOUS IN its simplicity compared to all other conventional sales training materials available, and initially, even a little crazy to those who have spent years investing in, or selling, the latest sales training on the market. But rest assured, there *is* sophistication in simplicity. It has taken me three years to simplify this sales checklist, which I now share with you.

Having been in the sales training industry for the better part of twenty years, I've observed countless companies reimplement their sales training or pursue the next shiny thing. This is not simply ongoing sales skills development and optimization; this is the belief that their overall sales process isn't yielding the desired results. Every few years they feel the need to start over "and do it right this time." Why do organizations continually do this? This always troubled me; something was fundamentally flawed. Was the training they invested in flawed? What was the root cause? Seeking the answer to this led to the writing of *The Sales Checklist*™.

There are many outstanding sales skills programs available. They teach how to ask questions, plan sales calls, handle objectives, pursue complex sales, manage key accounts, make presentations, and so forth. The reality is that most salespeople have an acceptable level of skills. Can they get better? Absolutely. Is it the real performance problem sales organizations are facing? No.

From our research, the average closing (conversion) percentage today, across all industries, is approximately 25%. This means that three out of four of the sales pursuits that make their way through your sales process will result in a loss, no decision, or an unknown conclusion.

Disappointingly, this losing rate is the same as it has been for many years. With access to so many sales skills programs, why is this happening?

What does this mean to your business or commission? Simply, you're losing money.

Why do we accept this? Any other department within your organization would consider this an abject failure. Would accounting be satisfied if 75% of billing was inaccurate? Would shipping consider 75% of deliveries being damaged a success? Of course not.

Our research has also shown that sales are lost every day not because the salesperson lacked skills such as questioning, presenting, or call planning; most salespeople have had basic sales skills training. The reason that sales are lost, or pursued when they should not be, is that the salesperson missed something that he or she knew they had to do. Why did they miss it? Because in the real world, it may be something they don't consistently execute. However, there are required steps that must be systematically covered to ensure a positive outcome—either a closed sale or an informed, early disengagement.

## WANT PROOF?

## The #1 Challenge to Every Sales Organization: THE CASE STUDY QUESTION

*Think of a critical, competitive sales opportunity where it's unclear if you're going to win or lose. Write that sale up as a case study, then hand it out to each member of your sales team, managers, and corporate leadership and ask, "What's the next best step to move this toward a close?"*

How many different answers would you get?

The answer we invariably get is, "The same as the number of people who review it!"

How does this variation in execution impact you and your organization?

What would be the impact on your sales organization, or your commission, if the answer was just one?

The reason companies continually reinvest in sales training is the fact that they are still losing approximately three out of four sales and that they don't have a satisfying answer to the Case Study Question.

The variation in sales execution leads directly to an unacceptably high defect rate and a tremendous waste of resources. Additionally, this variation also applies to the coaching of salespeople; if there isn't agreement on what to do next, effective coaching is nearly impossible.

So, how do we get to just one answer? How do we minimize variation in execution, defects, and waste? Utilize a checklist designed specifically for salespeople and sales organizations.

We know you're thinking a couple of thoughts.

First, "That's great, but we're different." Actually, sorry, you're not. Granted, there are nuances within different verticals and cultures. There are differences in how people sell within healthcare versus manufacturing versus business services, for example. However, just as accounting, quality control, and shipping processes are the same, so is the sales checklist.

Second, "Alright, but just how are you going to do this in the next two or three hours that it will take me to read this book?"

You might not believe me right now when I tell you it's easy, but read on and I will show you.

# THE SALES CHECKLIST™ — GET IT RIGHT EVERY TIME!

CHECKLISTS MINIMIZE AVOIDABLE FAILURES DUE TO LACK of attention, memory, or thoroughness. They empower professionals to have a higher baseline of performance by reminding them of the necessary steps in a process where missing one step potentially has the same consequences as missing all of the steps.

Although we don't typically think of a shopping list as a checklist, it is. Without a checklist, we forget to pick up items that we know we should. A checklist for shopping ensures you don't have to go back to the store to pick up the milk!

In aviation, checklists are vitally important, and pilots use them as part of their protocol because they have found that it could mean the difference between life and death.

The first known use of a checklist for pilots occurred following the 1935 maiden flight of the prototype Boeing XB-17 (later B-17) WWII bomber. The flight, conducted by one of the Air Force's most experienced pilots, ended in tragedy shortly after takeoff; the pilot forgot to release a locking mechanism on the rudder and elevator controls. The pilot knew he had to do it, but he simply missed a step. Once Boeing identified the cause of the crash, they developed a checklist to ensure that going forward, pilots didn't miss any steps.

Once the checklist was adopted, the impact was two million flying miles without a similar incident.

*Flight controls? Check. Flap settings? Check. Transponder? Check.*

How do we as salespeople and sales leaders gain the same consistency of a pilot successfully executing a flight from departure to arrival? How do pilots get it right statistically almost 100% of the time? How do they apply their knowledge consistently and correctly *every time*? How do they make the preflight look so easy, so simple? How do they manage extreme complexity so consistently? Simple, they follow a checklist.

When pilots follow the checklist and they identify a problem, do they view that as a failure? Of course not, they are just doing their job. It isn't good or bad, it's just data. The checklist allowed them to identify a problem that potentially could have put their flight at risk, which prompted them to take the appropriate corrective action. Shouldn't we in sales benefit from the same level of data-based decision making?

Another example of the power of checklists is in healthcare, as detailed in Dr. Atul Gawande's book, *The Checklist Manifesto*.[1]

Dr. Atul Gawande identifies three types of human failure:

1. Failure of memory (forgetfulness—too many steps to remember)
2. Failure of attention (tendency to forget boring or routine tasks)
3. Skipping steps that don't matter (sometimes harmless, sometimes disastrous)

In 2001, doctors at the Johns Hopkins Hospital were provided with a checklist for inserting tubes into chest cavities. The goal was to reduce the high rate of infections and yield more positive patient outcomes.

The checklist? You're probably imagining an elaborate, highly technical checklist that only a physician with years of schooling and training could understand. In reality, it was a five-step checklist that appeared so simple and easy to use that it certainly would not have any measurable impact. In fact, many people thought it was foolish to create a list for something the doctors and nurses had been taught for years. There was nothing that was new or complex on the checklist at all.

---

[1] Atul Gawande, *The Checklist Manifesto: How to Get Things Right* (New York: Henry Holt & Co, 2009), 240.

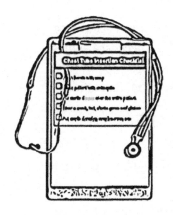

The checklist:

1. Wash hands with soap.
2. Clean the patient with antiseptic.
3. Put sterile drapes over the entire patient.
4. Wear a mask, hat, sterile gown, and gloves.
5. Put sterile dressing over the insertion site.

After one month of tracking just these five simple steps, studies showed that "in more than a third of the patients, they (the medical staff) skipped at least one (of the five)." These lapses, or human failures, were a result of memory or attention issues, skipping steps, or a combination of these.

Once the checklist was adopted:

1. Central infection rates in ICUs decreased by 66%.
2. Nurses felt empowered to bring up missed steps and say, "You didn't forget your mask, did you, Doctor?"
3. Hospital leadership felt empowered. Through the use of a checklist, it was discovered that chlorhexidine soap, which was the best at reducing infections, was available in less than one-third of the ICUs. Additionally, full sterile drapes often weren't available. The checklist enabled them to intelligently assign the necessary resources to address specific problems.

In short, the checklist minimized variation in execution, reduced the defect rate (infections), and reduced waste by promoting a more effective application of resources.

Checklists are efficient, to the point, and easy to use—whatever the situation. They don't tell you how to fly an airplane or how to perform surgery, but rather, they provide reminders of the most critical and important steps—the ones that even a pilot with fifteen thousand flight hours in a particular aircraft could miss. Pilots know that their training, experience, and judgment are not enough. They also know that missing steps, even simple ones, often produce devastating outcomes.

Salespeople, like pilots and surgeons, are overall competent and know how to ask questions, probe, develop solutions, develop coaches or mentors, and so forth. The reality, however, is that majority of their time (75% losing rate) is wasted on opportunities where they have missed a step or more. This leads to lost sales, or sales that were never going to be won being pursued to the end of the customer's buying process, which represents a tremendous opportunity cost.

Typically, customers require three to four companies to quote, or bid, on any major purchase. This means that the customer must motivate two or three of the salespeople who are not going to win the order to stay engaged in order to ensure they receive the necessary number of quotes. Using *The Sales Checklist*™ will ensure that you have visibility when you're the third or fourth quote, empowering you to make an informed decision whether to stay engaged or invest your resources where they will produce a greater return.

# MAKING THE CONNECTION BETWEEN SELLING AND CHECKLISTS

SALESPEOPLE, LIKE PILOTS AND SURGEONS, OPERATE IN a complex environment. The cost of missing a step or a detail may not be life-threatening, but they are a distinct threat to the health of your organization and your commission.

A sales checklist minimizes avoidable failure. No longer will missed steps lead to being blindsided by a surprise lost sale.

Checklists minimize avoidable failures due to lack of attention, memory, or thoroughness.

When nurses feel that they have the knowledge (the checklist) and the authority to bring up missed steps, they are less hesitant to do so. The impact is that everyone on the surgical team is engaged in providing positive patient outcomes—the same applies to your company. Sales, marketing, sales support, and leadership will be engaged and feel empowered to help deliver successful outcomes: increased sales.

You will immediately realize three outcomes by utilizing a sales checklist:

## MINIMIZED VARIATION IN SALES EXECUTION AND SALES COACHING

You will get one answer to the Case Study Question, thereby minimizing variation in sales execution and sales coaching.

A sales checklist will ensure that, like pilots or surgical teams, you don't miss steps, even the simple ones.

Why do steps get skipped? First, a salesperson simply forgets the step. Second, experience—either too little, not knowing what to do, or too much, becoming complacent. Third, salespeople who have a technical component to their job often stay within their comfort zones and instead focus on the science over the selling.

## REDUCED DEFECTS
Defects, or lost sales or sales pursued that are not going to close, will be minimized. Data, not gut feelings, will allow you to make informed decisions to continue to pursue a sale or to disengage and invest your sales resources where they will produce a greater return.

## REDUCED WASTE
Just as the leadership in the Johns Hopkins Hospital was empowered to make non-emotional, informed decisions as to the optimum manner to allocate resources, salespeople, sales leadership, corporate leadership, and marketing leadership will be able to make the same informed decisions to identify and prioritize where to optimally invest resources. This will ensure that resources are applied where they will produce the greatest return.

Not only will you be able to more intelligently apply your sales and marketing resources, you will also have additional resources available that previously were being wasted on opportunities that were not going to close.

## A PERSONAL NOTE TO YOU WHO ARE...

**Sales leaders** who are tired of struggling with the difficulty of growing sales organically, while managing and coaching salespeople who all seem to have their own ways of selling, to sales methodologies that consistently fail to meet your expectations. You're frustrated with low closing rates, inaccurate forecasts, wasted resources, and surprise losses. You've also likely invested in a CRM tool only to be disappointed with its adoption and impact. You're tired of the questions that you cannot comfortably answer.

- You'll learn how to implement a simple checklist, one that will empower you to run your sales territory or organization with the confidence and consistency of a pilot or a surgical team. Simple solutions get adopted, complex ones do not.

- Sales meetings, sales coaching, and deal reviews will be short, focused, productive, and consistent.

- Data will enable your team to systematically disengage from business they're not going to win. Do the math: If using the checklist empowers your sales team to intelligently fire one out of four of your pursuits and replace it with one more likely to close, how will your numbers be impacted? All of a sudden, a 10% plus growth in organic sales is very reasonable.

**Salespeople** who are tired of attending the "flavor of the month" sales training programs every year or two, only to have it be essentially forgotten in a few months. For this reason, many of you have become jaded and don't take new training seriously. I get that—I used to be one of those people who provided it to you!

- In the short time it takes to read this book, you'll learn a framework to consistently navigate any business-to-business sale, with no long implementation process. This book is written from a sales leader's point of view, but the concepts also apply to everyone within an organization.

- It will provide you with immediate, measurable results, including higher commissions.

**Sales trainers** who are feeling the pressure to add tools that quickly and measurably increase sales effectiveness, without the need to throw out or cannibalize what you have in place. You can no longer justify continually making large investments in training that don't meet expectations.

- You'll gain recognition for providing your team a tool that is easy to use, easy to coach, and immediately produces measurable results.

- You'll also gain recognition for quickly and cost-effectively optimizing your previous investments in sales training.

- You'll be able to train your team without them having to be out of the field for days at a time.

**Corporate leaders** who now realize that your sales organization is failing 75% of the time—this is no longer acceptable.

You're now beginning to think, "How *would* my organization be impacted if we could run our sales organization with the same level of consistency and predictability that a sales checklist can provide? Maybe we actually can get significantly more effective at selling."

- You'll be empowered to intelligently engage in any sales conversation. You'll have a checklist that provides you with the confidence of the captain of an airplane; you'll be able to lead sales strategy conversations. From these conversations, you will be able to make informed decisions on where to invest resources, and conversely, where not to. Variability in execution, defects, and waste will be consistently and systematically reduced in your sales department, just as you strive to do with your overall organization.

To all of you who are directly or indirectly involved in sales and seeking a simple yet sophisticated tool to immediately improve your sales results, we bring you:

**The Sales Checklist™**
**Get It Right Every Time!**

*www.thesaleschecklist.info*

# WHERE IT ALL BEGINS

LEARN ALONG WITH STEVE DURING HIS FIRST THREE months as the vice president of sales at a midsized manufacturing company called NST, Inc., based in St. Paul, Minnesota.

NST produced machine tools and robotic systems used by manufacturing companies. Steve, based in St. Louis, Missouri, was NST's top-performing salesperson during his seven years with the company. He always made or exceeded his quota and held close relationships with key accounts and distributors. But overseeing and coaching a team of fifty salespeople to reach their quota presented a different set of challenges, and the promotion required Steve and his wife, Sally, to relocate from St. Louis to St. Paul.

Joe, the founder and president of NST, was extremely focused on growing the skill set of everyone within his organization. He had invested significant resources in training over the years, especially for sales. This included questioning skills, probing, negotiating, selling value, lead generation, call planning, and consultative selling. Additionally, he had purchased multiple different sales processes or methodologies. However, the sales team was still experiencing unexpected losses, inaccurate forecasts, and every salesperson selling his or her own way.

A disciple of the world-renowned management consultant W. Edwards Deming, Joe believed that "if you don't have a process, you don't know what you're doing." Joe knew what every department was doing, except sales, and was committed to redressing the situation. His first corrective action was promoting Steve into the VP role.

Steve's euphoria about the new position was beginning to fade with awareness of the new sales challenges that need to be overcome. As he realized the magnitude of his new responsibilities, they started weighing heavily on him.

# IDENTIFYING THE PROBLEM

It was April 5, 6:00 AM, on a crisp, clear Minnesota morning. The alarm on Steve's phone could be heard echoing through the house. It was his and Sally's first morning in their new home. There would be many firsts for Steve today, first day in Minneapolis, first commute to the NST headquarters in St. Paul, and his first meeting with Joe as the new VP of sales.

*I wonder what Joe has planned?* Steve thought. *I have my own to-do list, but what could he add that he didn't mention over the last few weeks?*

Steve arrived at the office early, just after the lobby assistant. The building was three stories tall and Steve's office was on the third floor. Moving boxes didn't seem to bother him today. This was the start of something new. He was no stranger to the NST building, he'd been there many times before, mainly for training events or national sales meetings. But now, it had a new feel to it. His office view of the Mississippi River was certainly a step up from what he had back in Missouri—it was beautiful and was the first thing Steve admired as he walked into his new office.

By 7:58 AM, Steve was on his way to Joe's office. "Good morning, Steve!" said Joe excitedly. "Coffee?"

"Thanks, Joe, that would be great!"

"Steve, welcome to Minneapolis. You know how I feel about meetings, so let's cut to the chase. Sales is the only department in the company that I truly can't get my arms around. I have never been comfortable with the idea that sales is "different", and as long as we met our numbers, I just left it well enough alone. I can't do this anymore. The market is changing and getting even more competitive, sales are flat, and our resources are being strained. You know what a supporter I am of Deming and LEAN Six Sigma—I'm constantly focused on reducing the variability, defects, and waste in our processes. I think that we must do the same with our sales process, and this is where you come in."

Joe pulled out a notepad and began to write while he continued to talk.

"My vision of sales is very specific, very simple. In order to increase sales, you must accomplish three objectives."

Joe pulled a piece of graph paper out of his notepad. He preferred using graph paper to the typical legal pads as it made it easier to keep his notes in order—it appealed to his desire for everything to follow a process, a system. He began to write.

"First, minimize the variability in execution of the sales team; every salesperson must pursue opportunities the same way, and every manager must coach the same way, rather than everyone having their own system—that's just not manageable!"

Joe continued, "Second, our defect rate in sales is unacceptable."

*"Here are my goals for you, Steve."*

"What do you mean by defect rate?" Steve asked. "It's not like sales produces a product."

Joe responded, "By defects, I mean sales that are lost. As you know, our closing rate is about 25%. That means our defect rate is 75%. A defect is a lost sale, or a sale that we pursued to its conclusion even though we never had a reasonable chance at winning it. We're not the low-cost producer, you know. I know we can never win 100%, but I also know there are many very marginal pursuits we should walk away from. We can't afford to buy business, especially when there are so many accounts that we don't even call on."

Joe added another objective to the list. "Third, you need to make certain that our resources are applied where they will yield the greatest outcomes. We're wasting resources on opportunities that are never going to close. I understand that our salespeople have a very technical aspect to their jobs, but I'm tired of seeing so many 'science projects' in engineering."

> **Steve's Objectives:**
>
> 1) Minimize the variability in execution of the sales team
>
> 2) Reduce our defect rate in sales
>
> 3) Stop wasting company resources

Joe tore out the page and slid it across the desk.

Steve knew what each objective meant, but he wasn't sure how to achieve them and was glad he didn't need to give Joe something on the spot. Steve thought to himself, *That's not what I was expecting. I thought Joe put me in this position because of my selling abilities.*

"Joe, if you had to choose one, which do you think is the top priority?" he asked.

"I believe that if we solve the first objective, the rest will fall into place," said Joe.

Steve thought for a moment, wondering to himself if he was the right fit for the job. Finally, he asked Joe, "I'm very excited about this position, but frankly, I thought your goals would be for me to help minimize the commoditization we're facing, grow sales by a certain percentage, add new hires to our sales team, develop new sales aides—basically, get the sales team to sell like I sell."

Joe responded, "Do you have a question, Steve?"

Steve, feeling that maybe he should not have gone down this road, decided it would be best to get it out now, "Yes, I do. Why did you select me for this job?"

Joe chuckled and said, "That's a fair question, Steve. I would have been disappointed if you didn't ask it. I selected you because you ask questions like this. You have all the tools, the sales skills; you're just not applying them consistently. But I have observed that you continually try new ways to be an even better manager and salesperson. To be successful in this role, one must have the selling skills of a top performer, but also not be satisfied with the status quo. We have other salespeople and regional managers with much more experience than you. And I can tell you more than one was disappointed that they didn't get the position. But they are set in their ways. The message I get from them is, 'I've been selling this way for over twenty years. I'm successful. Why should I change?' You might say that they're encumbered with experience. I can't put my finger on it, but sales is the only department where I don't consistently have a good idea of what's really going on. Without this, I can't be of much value. I believe you can fix these problems. Does that answer your question?"

"Yes, it does, Joe. Thank you."

The day went by faster than Steve had anticipated. On his way home, he admired the neighborhood and pulled into the driveway. His next-door neighbor gave him a friendly wave through an open garage door. Not ready to unpack boxes yet, Steve decided to stop by and introduce himself.

"Hi! I'm Steve. We just moved to Minnesota, and we're next door to you."

"Nice to meet you, Steve. I'm Wally and this is my assistant, Dudley." Steve looked at the recliner and saw a friendly old black and white spotted cocker spaniel wagging his tail. "Welcome to the neighborhood. By the way, Steve, it's pronounced Minnesooooota!"

Steve replied, "Huh?"

*"Some call it a garage, the IRS and I call it The Boathouse."*

"Sorry, never mind. Where did your family move from?"

"Oh, well, nice to meet you, Wally, and you too, Dudley! We moved from St. Louis, Missouri, thanks to a work promotion at NST. By the way, that's pronounced Mizzura!"

Wally laughed at Steve's joke. "Well, congratulations on the promotion! I've heard great things about NST."

Steve glanced through the garage workshop, admiring Wally's tools neatly arranged on pegboards and obviously in a very well thought-out, systematic order. It was the combination of a woodworking shop and an operating room. He was immediately hit with the smell of spar varnish and wood shavings. He found it very calming.

"This is a great workshop. If I had to guess, I'd say you're a woodworker."

"Yes, I build wooden boats as a hobby and spend most of my time here, or on nearby lakes. I'm recently retired, so now I get to spend most of my time here building wooden boats and relaxing in my recliner, or more accurately, relaxing in my recliner and periodically building boats."

Steve chuckled. "Congratulations on the retirement!"

"Well, thank you very much! Retirement is a status I'm still getting used to, but Dudley figured it out a long time ago!" said Wally, nodding to the dog that was napping on the recliner.

"What line of work were you in?" Steve asked.

"I started my career as an engineer over at Mille Lacs Outboard Motor Company. It's a manufacturer of boat motors. I somehow ended up running the place by the time I retired." Wally didn't need to mention that in his fifteen-year tenure as company president, he grew the company from fifteen million to five hundred million in revenue.

Steve noticed rolls of blueprints and the long, thin wooden rowing oars in the corner. "Hey, my dad does a lot of woodworking and he's taught me how to use all of the tools, but I've never really built anything. I know a spoke shave from a block plane, but I could never build a boat. It seems much too complex for me. I wouldn't know what to do, or how to do it."

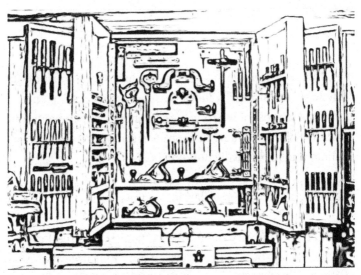

*"Having the tools, materials, and skills alone isn't enough. In order to build a boat, one must know how to build a boat."*

"It's simple, just follow the checklist that's on the blueprint. A checklist takes something complicated, like building a wooden boat, and breaks it down into simple, easy-to-execute steps. It ensures that anyone building this boat will end up with one that looks and functions just as the designer intended, with no variation. Follow the checklist and you won't miss any steps; you'll get it right every time. I'll be starting a new rowing shell tomorrow night. If you'd like to come by and see how to begin, I'd be happy to show you," said Wally.

"That would be great! I'd better get next door and help my wife, Sally, unpack. See you tomorrow!"

The next evening, after finishing unpacking for the night, Steve decided to take Wally up on his invitation and wandered next door. "Good to see you, Steve. Welcome to my shop—The Boathouse. I'm just starting. Take a look at the blueprint for me. What's the first thing on the checklist?"

Steve walked over to the well-worn workbench and paused as he looked over the blueprint. His first thought was that of complexity; the blueprint was overwhelming, but focusing on the checklist, he quickly realized the steps were easily identified.

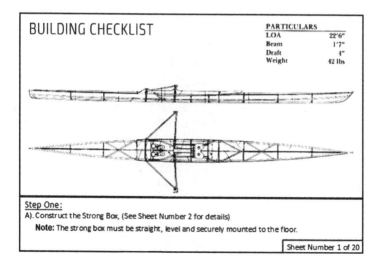

"Well, it says to prepare a strong box. What is that?"

Wally walked behind the neat stack of wood—every shape, size, and type of wood imaginable. "Well, it looks like a long table," he shouted. "The checklist says it needs to be straight, level, and securely mounted to the floor as the shell is built on top of it. That's the first step that anyone building this boat will do, with no variation. Do you see the description on the checklist?"

Steve examined the checklist while Wally peeked out from behind the wood. "Tell me how your day went. How's the transition to Minneapolis? I'm sure you're ready to dive into the role."

"I was so excited to get the promotion, but now reality is setting in, and I think I might be in over my head. I'm now the VP of sales. I've been with NST for seven years, so I'm no stranger to the organization and how we do things. However, we're facing increased commoditization of our business, new competitors, and an aging salesforce." Steve sighed. "I don't mean to dump this on you, Wally."

Wally smiled and silently thought back to his days in leadership—years of hiring, managing, and dismissing managers who didn't perform. He knew what kind of stress Steve was under. The average tenure for a VP of sales is only a couple of years, sometimes fewer if sales aren't turned around. There was always more turnover in sales leadership than any other part of the organization.

"I'm no stranger to your situation, Steve. I used to be the guy setting and establishing the growth goals."

"Speaking of setting goals, I have tremendous respect for Joe, our president. He built this company from the ground up and is driven to create an organization that is the hallmark of the industry, all while creating a positive work environment. He's more committed to supporting his team than I've seen with anyone in any other organization. I once asked him, 'Joe, aren't you worried when you spend all these resources on training and growing people that they may leave?' His response floored me: 'I'm more concerned that if I don't help them grow and develop, they'll stay.' Needless to say, I have big shoes to fill now that I'm managing the entire team."

"It sounds like a great opportunity for you. I'm certain Joe had his reasons for the promotion. So, what happened to the former VP of sales?"

"He was let go just shy of his three-year anniversary. He was a good guy, and we got along great. He was involved in every sale, but it just didn't scale. If salespeople are not trained to all sell the same way, Joe's vision for sales is not possible. Fifty salespeople are a lot if you're being 'superhero' in every deal. The team periodically hit the quarterly forecast, but many forecasted sales didn't close, and others that were not forecasted did. Joe is tired of being blindsided by lost orders, and he feels that sales is the only area of his company where everyone is doing things their own way. My predecessor invested in the same sales training he'd used in his last organization. We made a huge investment, and initially it seemed to work, but over a few months it just slowly went away. We still use bits and pieces of it, but not consistently."

Wally peeked out from behind the rack. "You want something to drink? Water? Soda?" There was a short pause from both of them. "Maybe a beer?" Wally asked.

"A beer would be great, thank you."

"Perfect! Do you like Grain Belt?"

"Grain Belt? Is that a microbrew?"

"Microbrew? No! It's a beer! It's a Minnesota classic—you'll love it!"

Wally brought the two ice-cold beers over to the workbench where Steve was now sitting.

"If Joe wants process, I'm guessing he's given you some objectives to achieve."

"Yes. In fact, I was given direction yesterday morning. Joe has assigned me three objectives."

Wally picked up a stub of a pencil and prepared to write on an open section of the blueprint.

"First, he wants me to eliminate the variability in execution of the sales team. Second—"

"What does Joe mean by this?" Wally interrupted.

"He shared with me that every department has a set way of

doing things, except sales. For example, if everyone taking orders over the phone in customer service did it their own way, the business couldn't function; maybe some, but not everybody, would get the right service. Joe doesn't like surprises, and we tend to get blindsided by sales pursuits that we feel are going to close but ultimately don't. He likes to identify best practices and enable everyone to do these the same way. Whenever Joe attends the regional sales meetings, he sees each manager has their own way of running the discussions."

"So today, salespeople all sell their own way? Don't you have a sales process?" asked Wally.

Slightly defensive, Steve responded, "Yes, we have a sales process."

"What are the steps?"

"It's pretty straightforward. First, we get a lead. Then, we qualify the lead, make a presentation, develop a proposal, often do a demonstration, and then we close," said Steve.

"Steve, if everyone does things their own way, you DON'T have a sales process!" Wally exclaimed.

He then wrote on the blueprint:

*Steve's Objectives:*

*1) Minimize the variability in execution of the sales team.*

"The second objective is to reduce our defect rate in sales. Joe views our 25% closing rate as a 75% defect rate. I don't know, I think every company has about the same closing rate."

"What's Joe's definition of defects?"

"He believes that any sale that is lost, or pursued when the facts don't warrant it, is a defect. He's concerned about how we waste resources and also the opportunity cost—I know he feels that there are many opportunities, including net new customers, that we don't have the time to pursue because of the time we spend on defects."

"So, what I'm hearing is that your *sales process* doesn't work about 75% of the time," said Wally, emphasizing sales process with air quotes.

Realizing he was coming on somewhat strong, Wally added the second objective and moved the conversation forward:

## 2) Reduce our defect rate in sales.

"Sounds reasonable so far. What's the third objective?" asked Wally as he continued writing the objectives on the corner of the blueprint.

"The third objective is to stop wasting company resources on sales opportunities that are not likely to move forward. For example, currently we need two additional application engineers to handle the backlog of demos and part runoffs. Joe doesn't think we need them. He said we need to eliminate the 'science projects.'"

"Science projects?" Wally asked.

"Yes, our salespeople need to have strong technical skills to do their jobs. Joe feels that many of the projects we work on are never going to go anywhere, so he calls them science projects."

Wally added the final objective:

### 3) Stop wasting company resources.

Wally asked Steve, "What does success look like for Joe?"

"Joe likes yes and no answers. No maybes. No gray areas. He's very specific about this. He thinks we'll achieve our goal when I can select one of our critical, competitive, active sales opportunities where the outcome is in doubt, write it up as a case study, and hand it out to each member of the sales team, including the managers and myself. That's over fifty people. Then I'd ask, 'What's the next best step to moving this sale toward closing?' Success is when we get the same answer from everyone on the sales team."

Wally put down his beer and picked up the pencil to write "One Answer," then circled it under the three objectives.

"I think this seems reasonable. How do you feel?" Wally seemed relatively unphased by what he heard. Having been in Joe's position, he could empathize with Joe.

"Well, it's not what I expected. I thought he promoted me because I've been a top producer for three years and I could get the other salespeople to sell more like I do."

*Steve's Objectives:*
1) *Minimize the variability in execution of the sales team*
2) *Reduce our defect rate in sales*
3) *Stop wasting company resources*

One Answer

"So, Steve, you say you have a sales process, but everyone is doing things their own way, you're losing most of the time, and you're misapplying resources, is that right?"

"Yes, but—"

"What do you think the problem is, Steve?" Wally interrupted.

"Initially I was excited about this position," Steve responded. "But then I started thinking that I can't be everywhere all the time. I always made my number, but now I'm responsible for everyone's. I can't physically help each salesperson close every order," stressed Steve.

"For the most part, my sales team is very experienced. We have a few salespeople with under five years of selling, but we're definitely a tenured organization. In fact, about a third are going to retire in the next five years. They work hard—that's never been the problem. You might say we're encumbered by experience.

Many of our salespeople spend too much time where they are the most comfortable, for example, on the technical nature of our solutions, and also too much time with the same customers. They don't spend enough time on the selling aspect of their role. I used to wrestle with the same thing. I think we need to improve our selling skills, but I'm not sure if some of the older salespeople will be open to more training. I'm hesitant to really shake the tree and mix things up. The last thing I want to do is negatively impact the results."

"What concerns do you have when working with Joe on these objectives?" asked Wally as he pointed to the list in front of Steve.

"He's a great guy to work for. I knew how to make him happy when I was selling, but as the sales VP, I don't know how I'll be able to pass his 'one answer' vision. On top of that, he doesn't believe the solution lies in taking what we've done in the past and improving on it. He seems to feel there is some underlying problem that we have not been able to identify. He's all about process and systems, he just doesn't understand that sales is an art. It's about relationships."

"Is selling an art?" Wally couldn't hold himself from asking.

"Of course, it is! Haven't you heard of a natural-born salesperson, or a salesperson who could sell ice to Eskimos?" asked Steve.

"I guess I never really understood that. Art doesn't seem to be repeatable. Gertie, my better half, works on a pottery wheel.

She can throw a pot with the best of them, but she never seems to be able to perfectly replicate the same one. So anyway, what's your first step?"

"We did sales training about three years ago, right when the former VP took his position. He was hired from outside the company, and I think he got the job by telling Joe all about the training he'd implemented at other companies. But we just didn't stick with the material. I thought I'd do something similar, but this time, we'll do it right on my watch. I've been with the company for almost seven years. I have a better feel for what we need. I'll make it stick. But that plan changed today—Joe doesn't want to try to fix our problems with something we've tried in the past."

"What do you mean 'do it right this time'?" asked Wally.

"Well, the last sales training at NST was good, and the presenter was really entertaining. Everyone loved his stories and humor, but we just didn't follow through with the material. It was difficult to get salespeople to use it once the workshop was over. The material was solid, though. I think most salespeople thought that if they just waited a couple of months, the whole training would be forgotten."

"Was it forgotten?"

"Well, for the most part, I guess. We still used a lot of the language and some of the key elements, but yes, for all practical purposes, it was forgotten."

"How about we start laying out the strong box? Based on the checklist, we know the wood that we need to use. I'll pull it from my wood rack and you can put it on those sawhorses I have set up by the workbench."

"Yes, that sounds good, Wally. I'm anxious to see how you do this!"

# REALITY SETS IN

STEVE SPENT THE NEXT TWO WEEKS SETTLING INTO HIS role and developing a routine. He was also contacted by four sales training companies; it seemed they assumed, with him being new, he would want to do things his own way.

A few weeks had passed. It was now Friday, and Steve was in the Houston airport waiting for his 6:26 PM flight to Minneapolis to begin boarding. He was disappointed to learn that the plane was a single-aisle commuter—for a three-hour flight!

It had been an interesting week with his Central South team. Steve found himself viewing his salespeople differently; he became frustrated and concerned. Sales conversations were drawn out and each sale that was discussed felt like throwing darts at a blank board. His key takeaway was that nobody seemed to be able to ask the right questions to get customers to take action.

Boarding for the flight began, and Steve was thirty minutes away from putting on his headphones and disengaging from the world around him.

*How do I hold short, strategic sales meetings? How can I get each regional manager to coach to any changes I implement? How do I create a buy-in? How does each salesperson realize that changes are going to help them be successful? How am I ever going to be able to accomplish my objectives?!* These concerns were swirling around his head when he finally drifted off to sleep. That is, until the person seated in front of him lurched his chair back into full recline, spilling Steve's beverage and knocking his Bischoff's cookies to the floor.

*"Seriously?!"*

By the time the flight landed in Minneapolis, Steve was more than ready for the respite that the weekend would provide.

The next morning, he strolled over to Wally's. "Hard at work, I see!" said Steve as Wally had a rake in one hand and a bag full of leaves in the other.

"Ha! I'm almost finished," said Wally.

"Wally, I thought, if you weren't busy, I could get your thoughts on some things. Our talks a few weeks ago really helped."

"Of course! Come on over." The two met in the garage, and Wally was waiting at the table. "The last time you were in here, we talked about your three goals with Joe. I think you were going to put some thought into identifying how to fix those problems. How's that going?"

"Actually, it's not going well," Steve replied dejectedly.

Steve and Wally walked back into the shop. They sat on wooden stools, and Dudley was already lounging on the recliner.

"Steve, do me a favor, would you? Take off 1/32 of an inch off the top of this piece of cedar stringer—it's a little proud."

"Sure, which plane should I use?"

"Your choice! You know how to use the tools!"

"Hmmm, I'll use this number 4 block plane," said Steve.

Wally could see that the distraction was helpful for Steve; the tenseness was beginning to leave his face.

"You were beginning to tell me how it's going."

"Yeah, well, I'm struggling. I've been contacted by four sales training companies in the last two weeks. Some of their stuff sounds really interesting, but I know that Joe will not sign off on it. Plus, I still think the previous sales training we did was solid; it just didn't stick."

"Well, Steve, I'm not an expert, but the first thing I would do is identify the problem."

Steve was obviously enjoying the progress he was making on the stringer. With each long, smooth push of the plane, a long, thin, fragrant cedar chip was produced. Finally, Steve said, "I have three problems—variability, defects, and waste."

"Alright, Joe has given you three problems. What's common among them? Anything?"

"I'm not sure, but I did ask Joe which is the top priority, and he said that if I address the variability in execution, everything else would fall into place."

Changing the subject, Wally said, "I'll put some thought into it, but enough sales talk for this morning. How about you work on your boatbuilding skills?"

"Actually, that sounds great; it would be helpful to get my mind off business for a while." Steve seemed relieved. He realized that each time he talked to Wally, he had his own "aha" moment and gained a new perspective to his situation.

Wally got the rowing shell blueprint out. "Well, since you were last here, I built the strong box. Take a look at this red chalk line down the center where the shell is being constructed. What do you think it's for?"

"Looking at the blueprint, I see a piece of wood going from the front to the back. It's called the keel."

"Stem to stern! When we're using checklists and building boats, we need to use a common language to eliminate misunderstandings. What else does the checklist say?"

"That's easy. It says it's made from a 2-inch square piece of white oak and that it must be positioned perfectly straight, as the rest of the shell is built based on it."

The checklist was significantly easier for Steve to use this time. Anything new at first glance was complicated, but now he was able to apply it.

"Perfect! Now, what do you think would happen if the keel wasn't perfectly straight?" asked Wally as he inspected his work.

"The boat wouldn't go in a straight line; it would be turning all the time."

"That's right. If you were to see a boat that was constantly turning, no matter what the rower was doing, what do you think the problem is?"

"The problem is that the boat isn't going straight, right?"

"True, but what's causing the boat not to go straight? The boat's inability to go straight is a symptom. What do you think is the underlying issue...the root cause? The 'problem,' if you will? Just like we talked about regarding your sales situation."

Steve thought for a second. "Well, I'd say the keel isn't straight."

"Exactly! If you wanted to make the boat go straight, what would you do?"

"Simple, I'd fix the keel."

"Why not just add a rudder that would counteract the turning?"

"Because the turning isn't the problem; it's that the keel isn't straight. I'd want to fix problem, or I guess, as you would say, the root cause."

"And where would you find the information on what's required for the keel to be straight?"

"On the checklist, I suppose."

"Now you have it! One more question, once I've clamped the keel in place on the strong box, how will you know if it's in the right place?" asked Wally.

"Easy! It's either centered over the red center line or it isn't." Steve pointed to the red chalk line.

"We can agree that the keel is either straight or it isn't. There's no middle ground, right? No gray area. It's binary."

Steve agreed, and they laid the keel across the red chalk line.

"Right. But, Wally, what does all this have to do with selling?"

"Hypothetically, if we brought any one of your fifty salespeople, or Joe, into the Boathouse, and using facts instead of gut feelings, would they be able to tell you whether the keel was in the correct position or not?" Wally knew exactly where he wanted the conversation to go but was careful not to lead Steve too much.

"Yes, I appreciate that level of precision when it comes to boatbuilding, but I need to build a professional *sales* team. My salespeople need to sell more—it's not a boatbuilding problem. Anyway, I'd better get back home. I'll let you get back to your recliner, I mean work!" said Steve, somewhat flustered, but thankful.

On Steve's way out of the garage, Wally said very pointedly, "Steve, I'd say your sales problem is not a training issue—your boat isn't rowing straight. Conventional sales training alone won't fix the problem; it only treats the symptoms."

Steve looked back at Wally, wanting to ask for an explanation, but unsure of what to ask. Wally could see that Steve was frustrated, but he knew that he had to figure out the problem for himself. He knew the steps Steve must go through to ultimately identify the root cause and a solution.

The following Monday morning, Joe asked Steve to provide an update. It had been about a month since their first conversation. Steve knew this was going to be one of many sales reviews he would have with Joe. He was looking forward to it, but it was a new experience. He was feeling nervous and excited, but he also had a nagging feeling of being unprepared, of not knowing what he didn't know. His biggest concern was the sales forecast and pipeline he inherited. He always knew that forecasting was a guessing game based on gut feelings. But now, he was the one responsible.

Steve shared with Joe what he believed to be the best way to get sales back on track and meet their goals, which he felt was to reinvest in sales training. Steve believed he could implement the training in a manner that would allow him to accomplish Joe's goals. He also felt that it was from a safe, well-known brand name. But he added that he understood that Joe didn't see that as a solution.

"Steve, with all due respect, we've spent a fortune on sales training over the years. We've made investments for years. We're good at questioning, call planning, answering objections, presenting, and so forth, yet we're continually blindsided by losses. This would be our third new program in the last eight years. Granted each was new and offered additional insights, but..." his voice trailed off. "Steve, what's going to be different this time around? That's why, unless you can convince me, I don't feel we have a sales skills problem."

Steve left Joe's office with a sinking feeling in his gut. *What is he really saying to me? I need to make an impact, clean up our pipeline, get a quick return on new hires, and start coaching managers to their top opportunities. What have I gotten myself into? What a mess!*

Driving home after work, Steve crossed the Mississippi River over the 35W bridge. He looked down at University of Minnesota's rowing team practicing on the river—the long rowing shells, some with one rower, others with four, or even eight, all operating as one.

Then everything started to come together: *If a boat doesn't go straight, that's the symptom. The problem, the root cause, is that the keel wasn't laid straight. When Joe asked me why we weren't meeting our numbers, he was really asking what's the problem. What's keeping us from meeting his three objectives? What's keeping our shell from going straight? Why do we have to make continual corrections, retraining our sales team, to try and make our boat go straight? Why didn't the previous sales training work? The symptoms are the three objectives he's set for me, but the problem is SOMETHING. They all lead back to something...*

*"If a boat doesn't go straight...the keel wasn't laid straight!"*

# THE SALES CHECKLIST™

WALLY WAS WORKING ON THE SHELL WHEN STEVE WALKED in that evening. It was a beautiful evening for May; the snow banks were almost gone. Wally didn't have much of a choice but to work since his recliner was occupied by Dudley, who gave a friendly, halfhearted bark as Steve entered, then promptly returned to his nap.

"Wally, I think I know what you mean by the problem versus the symptom. A boat not going straight is the symptom of a keel problem, right?

"You got it," he feigned disinterest and continued with his head buried in the boat shell.

"Joe wanted to know why we're not meeting our numbers. I told him we needed to have our sales team trained, but I have a feeling I'm missing the boat, pun intended. It's a gut feeling, but...I'm close."

"Steve, can you give me a hand?"

"Sure, but I can't stay too long."

"Oh, it won't take long. What do you think the next step is on this boat?"

"Uh, Wally, I'm in a bit of a hurry." Steve wasn't in much of a boatbuilding mood, but since he walked in on Wally working, he went along.

"Look at the checklist. What does it say we need to do next to ensure we end up with a straight keel?"

Steve walked through the garage past the recliner to the blueprint that was on the workbench. He started at the top of the checklist to ensure he was in the right spot. They spent the next few minutes talking through the details of the next step. "Well, it says build the strong box, oh, we did that, let me see… um, it says to cut out bulkheads C from an 8-mm mahogany."

"Now that you know the 'what to do,' the 'how to do it' is very straightforward. That will ensure you end up with the outcome you're seeking. You're going to be a boatbuilder! When you're learning a new process such as building a wooden boat, there is a common language you have to learn. This helps remove variation," said Wally.

Walking to the other side of the workbench, Wally continued to make the connection between sales and boatbuilding. "So, back to your work situation, I didn't mean to cut you off, but let me ask you this—if you had fifty salespeople, I mean master carpenters, and gave them all the tools and materials to build a boat, would they be able to do it?"

"Sure, a master carpenter has all the necessary skills to do the job."

"I agree. They have the skills related to *how* to do things, but what good are their skills if they don't know *what* to do? You have woodworking skills, but can you build a rowing shell?"

"No, but—"

Wally cut Steve off, "How effective is a football player if he has the skills to play, but can't remember the playbook during the big game? If the carpenters have the skills but don't know what to do, will the boat be built correctly?"

"If the carpenters followed the checklist, yes. Just as if the football players followed the designed play, then yes."

"Aha! I didn't say they had the checklist or a playbook. I just said they had the skills, tools, and materials."

"Then I suppose they would fail."

"But what if I gave the carpenters the newest sales training, I mean, technical training, latest types of glue, fasteners, and tools? Would the outcome of the boat be perfect?"

"No, it doesn't matter what tools or training you give them if you don't start with the—" Steve stopped midsentence. "You got me! My salespeople are good carpenters, they just don't have a checklist! It's the same with me building the boat with you—I know how to saw, plane, sand, and fasten wood together, I just don't have the checklist or the blueprint to follow."

"Ha! Yes! The checklist ensures that the boat goes straight when we first put it in the water. It removes the variation, so everyone builds a shell that looks and functions as intended. It provides what's needed to coach someone building a boat. Even the coaching shouldn't have variation. Any other boatbuilder will guide you the same way I have," said Wally. "On top of that, you'll cut down on defects and wasted time and materials."

"So, if I put my salespeople through the sales training again, they're likely to sharpen their skills, but I'm not fixing the problem. We've done this sales training before, our boat is floating and moving, but isn't going straight. You realize what you're suggesting is 100% opposite from what every sales training company is saying, right?"

"Yes, I think that's the conclusion *you* just came to. If you did the sales training again, or the newest sales training on the market, that's the next shiny thing. You don't want to treat the symptoms—you want to fix the problem, the root cause. Any business issue can be separated into symptoms versus the root cause. Great leaders are able to separate the symptoms from the problem. We can't solve today's problems with the same solutions that caused them in the first place."

"Well, there isn't a checklist for selling—"

"I disagree. *You* have the checklist in your head. Successful, professional salespeople like you execute it at an unconscious, competent level. Trust me, you have one."

Steve took a long glance at the boat checklist. "Maybe this sales checklist might be what I'm looking for."

"Tell me again about your sales process. What are the steps you would typically go through?" asked Wally.

"First, we try to set an appointment for a qualification call, or discovery visit, with a lead or prospect. This lead could come from an online inquiry, marketing, a trade show, or a referral. Then we make a presentation, possibly perform a showroom demo, get their feedback, and prepare a proposal. Finally, we deliver the proposal and negotiate for the order."

"When your team follows these steps, what percentage of the customers you engage actually buy from you or turn into customers?"

"Joe says that overall, we're closing about 25% of our pursuits—the industry average."

"If you and I built four boats, and three of them didn't row straight, would that be acceptable to you? Would you think that we followed the checklist on the three boats that didn't row straight?" asked Wally. Not waiting for an answer, Wally continued, "If we spent all that time and materials on three boats that will never see the water, we certainly didn't follow the checklist. That sounds like a waste of resources."

Steve sat down on the wood stool next to the bench, holding the blueprint. He read over his three sales initiatives that Wally had written on it. "Wally, where would you start to design a checklist for selling?"

"I'm not a natural-born salesperson by any means, but the first place I'd start is what we've been discussing—the keel. How do we start out straight? Before one of your salespeople begins to invest resources in a sales pursuit or new opportunity, what's the first thing you want to know?"

"What do we need to do to win the order?" said Steve.

"Okay, but you just shared with me how your current sales methodology produces defects 75% of the time. In other words, you need to build four boats to get one good one. Perhaps thinking about winning isn't the best place to start?"

# THE SALES CHECKLIST™
# GET IT RIGHT EVERY TIME!

### 1) CUSTOMER FIT

"I think you know exactly where to start. You mentioned the first thing you would ask your salespeople about a pursuit: What do we need to do to close it? When I build a boat, I rely on the checklist to ensure that I lay the keel correctly *every time*, as the rest of the boat is lost without a solid foundation. Do you find that some customers are easier to close than others?" asked Wally.

"Sure," shrugged Steve. "There are easy ones and tough ones. But our salespeople are bulldogs, they never give up!"

"Is that a good thing?" Wally asked. "Are you everything to everyone, or do you have a sweet spot for certain types of people and organizations in the market? Let me say it this way: If you asked your sales team and managers to define your sweet spot, would they all provide the same answers?

Steve paused. "Well, no. I would probably get different responses."

"How do you think that impacts your sales effectiveness if your organization can't even agree on what makes for a good-fitting customer? What do you think would happen to your closing percentage if you had more opportunities from prospects or customers in your sweet spot, and fewer from those that are not?

In other words, how many boats in your pipeline don't have a straight keel? How can we avoid making those three defective boats that will never see the water?"

"That sounds great, but we pursue all opportunities. Sales is a numbers game. If we want to increase our sales, we need to increase our number of phone calls, quotes, and proposals."

Wally began pacing around the workshop, looking at the rowing shell structure from different angles. "I'll agree with you that it's a numbers game, but I think we're looking at different numbers. Does your sales team have every prospect covered in every territory? Are they getting all the low-hanging fruit from your existing customers?" he asked.

"Of course not, there isn't time."

Trying to hide his frustration, Wally added, "Then why invest time and resources on the ones that are not likely to close? What if your team could systematically disengage from those prospects or customers that are not a good fit and instead invest more time and resources on the ones that are a good fit for your organization?"

"I suspect our closing rate would increase and we'd have fewer surprise losses. But that's easier said than done. How do we know if we're not going to win? We all know we shouldn't spend time on losing sales, but we often just don't know until the customer makes a decision. I guess this is where experience and gut feelings come into the picture."

Wally couldn't hide his frustration from Steve. "Experience and gut feelings? Using gut feelings is what your team is doing now? Can you manage gut feelings? Can you coach gut feelings? Do they scale? Sure, my experience building rowing shells is a plus, but checklists are designed to replace gut feelings with accurate data—data that drives informed decision making."

Steve was somewhat taken back by Wally's reaction, but he also knew that he was right. He became even more concerned that he was in over his head.

Wally, sensing that he came on kind of strong, softened, "Do you remember when you first came here and said there was no way you could build a wooden rowing shell? Let's make a deal. You help me with this boat, and I'll help you develop a checklist for selling. We'll identify a way to increase your closing rate by identifying customers that are a good fit for you. This provides your sales team with a mini checklist you can use."

Wally moved the blueprint around on the table to where Steve had written Joe's three objectives for him. "Okay, here are Joe's three goals for you. Let's make our sales checklist. The first step is to identify if a customer is a good fit."

Steve wrote: "Sales Checklist" and "Fit."

"We lay a keel for a boat foundation; we're going to let customer fit be the first step on our checklist. It doesn't make sense to pursue someone if they're not a good fit! Do you think anyone on your sales team could identify the correct keel position?" asked Wally.

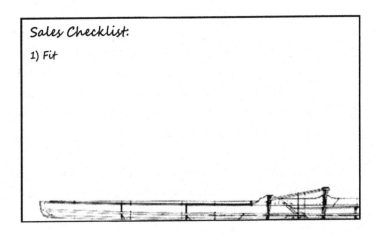

"Absolutely! It fits or it doesn't. Black or white. No gray area. It's either centered on the red chalk line or it isn't, simple!" Steve answered proudly.

"Any gut feelings or experience required to know if it's centered or not?" challenged Wally.

Steve responded enthusiastically, "No. I like that!"

"Right. This is how you will bring the same type of non-emotional, binary outcome to your sales team—either it is in the right position or it isn't. No maybes. No gut feelings. Do you think pilots will pull back from the runway if something on their checklist is a maybe? Of course not, well, unless they had a few cold ones before the flight!"

"That's terrible, Wally!" Steve chuckled.

Wally continued, "Let's start with the fit of your customers. Tomorrow, when you're in the office, analyze a number of important sales that were won and some that were lost. Come up with five criteria that make for a good fit. Maybe even come up with criteria that make for a bad fit, to compare. Then we can add them to your checklist."

Determined to answer Wally's question, Steve went into the office early the next morning to review his old sales successes, losses, and active pursuits. He noticed patterns at a deeper level than the typical customer characteristics on paper (such as location, industry type, and size of company). His findings were that for each of his successes (sales won), his prospect or customer was not solely a price buyer, they appreciated NST's brand and value-added services. Also, upon reflection, he realized that he could easily meet with most or all of the people involved in the decision-making process.

That's two, now he had to come up with three more and structure these criteria in a way that was easily binary and coachable.

The Minneapolis headquarters was home to three of Steve's salespeople, including Juanita. Juanita was in her first year at NST and had caught Steve's attention as someone who was very motivated to become a professional salesperson. Steve wanted to try out his mini checklist during his afternoon customer visits with Juanita, which consisted of a key customer meeting and a few initial discovery sales calls. Steve and Juanita met in his office thirty minutes before leaving.

Before Juanita arrived, Steve wrote down two fit criteria on an index card.

"I'm looking forward to our call this afternoon," said Steve as they sat down at his office conference table. Juanita, I'd like to get your thoughts on what characteristics make a customer a good fit for us. We can't be everything to everybody. We need to be able to identify customers that are a good fit and ones that are not. Make sense?"

"Sure, the ones who buy are good fitting customers!" said Juanita.

Knowing that she was only half joking, Steve felt he needed to make the point a little clearer. "Well, are they? Think about Bear Industrial in Chicago. They're a customer of yours. Have they been worth your time?"

"No! They're terrible to work with. We had to discount the order so much, it wasn't profitable. They don't pay their invoices, and they call me all the time with unrealistic demands and requests. They also said if we provided them with the special pricing and terms that they would be loyal to us. That lasted about a day... I wish I'd never sold them." Juanita's voice trailed off, and Steve could see that she had understood the point.

Steve handed Juanita the index card and said, "Here is the start of the list. Let's use this during our calls today. Speaking of our calls, what are we looking to accomplish?" It was an open question, but Steve wanted to see what type of response he'd get.

"We're meeting with a key customer, so I'm looking to touch base and see if we can move anything new forward." Steve had hoped for a more specific answer. *I believe that Juanita could be a top performer; she just needs coaching and an idea of what to do next...a checklist!*

They arrived at their meeting with Mark, the VP of manufacturing for Twin Manufacturing, a longtime client of NST and one that Juanita felt she could acquire a greater share of their annual spend.

Steve and Juanita waited for Mark in the lobby. Steve peered through the doorway into their fabrication shop and saw a LEAN Six Sigma poster. He also saw a poster of a go/no-go gauge with two columns titled "YES" and "NO" next to each instruction task. He admired the simplicity of the binary outcome—either one or the other; no maybes. It reminded him of Wally's comments about an airline pilot's checklist—absolutely no maybes. *Could sales be as simple as a go/no-go gauge,* he thought.

During the meeting, Mark brought in Tom, the new quality control manager. "Tom, I'd like to introduce you to Steve and Juanita from NST, a longtime partner of ours. Tom is our new QC manager. He's had some concerns on a job we're bidding on, and he needs your help. I've shared with him that you guys are a big help to us remaining competitive."

Steve did his best not to be the Superman sales VP who swoops in to be the hero and takes over every deal. He knew that for him to be able to manage fifty salespeople, Juanita had to drive the conversation.

Back in the car, as they headed back to the office, Steve asked Juanita how she thought it went.

"I thought it was great! They don't buy on price, we help them remain productive, and the key people are accessible, just like you shared with me!"

"I noticed that too. How many of your customers are like that?"

"Maybe a quarter of them. Why?"

"What do you think would happen to your territory if half of your customers were like Twin Manufacturing?"

"I think I'd win salesperson of the year! Maybe even be the next VP of sales!" said Juanita, half in jest.

Steve chuckled to himself thinking, *Careful what you wish for!*

Steve and Juanita continued their sales meeting review back in Steve's office.

"So now that the meeting has digested a bit, how do you think the afternoon went?" asked Steve.

Juanita let out a sigh. "I think it was okay, but looking back, I missed an opportunity."

"Tell me more," Steve said.

"Well, I forgot to ask about who is going to be involved with the proposal review. I know better! That's basic stuff. I can't believe I forgot!"

Steve replied, "Our sales are complex; it's easy to miss important steps, even when we know better."

On the way home that night, Steve drove past Wally's workshop and saw the lights on. He knew Wally could help him organize his thoughts, so he stopped by. "Wally, I'm close to understanding what makes a good fit. It was a great learning day for me," said Steve as he entered the workshop.

"Great, let's hear it," said Wally. He waved jokingly for Dudley to join the conversation, who looked up from *his* recliner with a look of don't you guys know what time it is in dog hours?

"I went back as you suggested and studied our major wins and losses. I found a couple of common factors. First, they appreciated our brand and value-added services; they didn't just buy on price. Second, we could meet with all the people involved in the decision-making process. These two areas were part of all the major company deals we won, whether it was a new customer or a repeat customer. This was also verified by a key customer's behavior today."

"Fantastic observations! Anything else?"

"Well, after riding along with one of my local reps, I realized two other elements that could be important, even vital. The people we met with, our decision influencers, are not only available to meet but also engaged. That was clear during an appointment today. We met with a company looking to purchase a new line of vertical machining centers with robotic loading. Our meeting was with a manufacturing engineer and we came up with a way to reduce the number of machines needed while increasing throughput. This would require a change to their specification. He just picked up the phone and called the VP of engineering. He said to come on down to his office and talk about it. By the time we left, he agreed to change the specification and was appreciative of our ideas. When we can meet with someone like that and get them to change the specification to our solution, that's a great sign.

Also, after an uncomfortable conference call with a prospect, I realized that anyone we work with must be open and honest. They had sent us a specification for a horizontal machining center and asked us to provide a quote. Based on this, my salesperson set up a conference call. She had asked to have engineering on the call, in addition to procurement, to ensure that we understood what they were trying to accomplish and that we could offer our best solution. They had agreed, but during the conference call, only procurement was available to be on it. The guy in procurement said that the engineer was tied up. We said that wasn't a problem and that we'd get the initial overview of the project from him and then set a follow-up call with the engineer. Instead, the procurement guy said he would just relay the information to the engineer and let us know if he had any questions. All he needed was the best price we could offer. I knew he wasn't being honest with us. We were just being used as column fodder."

"Column fodder?"

"Yeah, you know, he probably needed four quotes and we were the third or fourth column on his spreadsheet."

"Ha! I hadn't heard that one before! Well, that's four criteria. Do you have one more?"

"Well, ideally there would be a minimum size of sale; a small deal and a big deal almost take the same amount of work to win. So, ideally the sale should be over $100k."

Steve pulled the index card out of his pocket with the morning notes and added the additional criteria to the checklist.

*Fit Criteria:*

*A. Appreciates NST brand and value*

*B. All contacts are accessible*

*C. Contacts are engaged*

*D. Open and honest communication*

*E. Size - $100K minimum*

"Steve, how often do you think your salespeople are pursuing customers that don't meet at least three out of the five criteria?"

"I never looked at it that way. It has to be at least 25-30% of the time." Wally could see that Steve was processing that fact.

Steve finally said, "I know what you're going to ask next, and the answer is yes."

"What was I going to ask?"

"You were going to ask me about the impact if we focused more of our resources on good-fitting customers. Obviously, it will have a tremendously positive impact. Even if a customer or prospect just meets three of the five, it would be a tremendous help toward cleaning our pipeline and forecast. I imagine our pipeline is filled with some pursuits that may meet one of the criteria, possibly not any, yet we are still putting resources into them. It's just that we all have been taught that sales is a numbers game; the more you quote, the more you win."

"Exactly. Again, I'm not a sales guy," Wally said, his tongue firmly in his cheek. "But what if you took that list of five fit criteria and had your sales team score all their current pursuits against that. I'd want to know how many meet three or more of the fit criteria based on facts, not emotions. Let's say if they don't meet at least three, they get disqualified…unless there's a compelling reason to stay engaged."

"I love it! I saw a go/no-go gauge sign today, and it reminded me of Joe's desire for a yes-or-no outcome. You just called it a score, so let's put the two together." Steve wrote a "yes" box and a "no" box next to each fit criterion.

"Here's a question for you, Steve. What are all five criteria when you first start discussing an opportunity?"

"I'm not sure what you mean. Initially, we wouldn't know."

"Exactly, Steve, every criterion is a question mark until you can determine if it's a yes or a no. Let me ask you another question. Just suppose that you and I review an opportunity and determine that they fit all five criteria. Are you done with fit?"

"Well, if they're a fit, they're a fit."

"How long can your sales cycle be?"

"For some of our sales, it can be eighteen months, or even more."

"Is it reasonable that the company will go through changes during that time? Changes that may impact fit?"

"When you put it that way, yes," said Steve.

"I'd agree. It will make sense to review if an opportunity is a fit on a regular basis."

"I see where you're going, Wally. That makes sense. I'm going to write this up and send it out to my team tonight! We can leverage the yes-or-no element. It's either a fit or it isn't. Three out of five is our goal. Regardless of the score, it's just data. We can coach to a no. We may be disappointed when a pilot comes on the intercom and says we have an issue that needs to be checked out before we depart, but it beats the alternative...unless it's Friday night after a long week and I want to get home!"

Steve smiled as he walked back to his house that night, appreciative of his conversations and friendship with Wally.

The next day, Steve shared the customer fit criteria with his team. The launch of customer fit into NST's sales culture was an instant success. Each salesperson scored all of their active pursuits, and Steve found that roughly 20% of the pipeline met less than three of the fit criteria.

A week later, Steve arrived in the office at around 7:00 AM, anxious to update Joe. "Joe, we all now know exactly what makes for a good-fitting customer. No gut feelings, just data. We're now confidently either not engaging or firing about one out of five pursuits—20%! That's giving us additional selling time, and we've freed up a significant amount of application engineering resources. We're getting better at understanding that getting a no is often the right answer."

Joe responded, "Customer fit alone has had a greater, measurable impact than any sales training we've done before. Plus, it's quick and simple to use. Now, that, I can get my arms around!"

Steve was the most excited he'd been since taking on his new position. For the first time, Steve felt he was on the right track.

The next day, regional and one-on-one coaching calls were scheduled. Anyone in the sales organization, or the entire organization, for that matter, could use the customer fit and determine if the sale they were working on was a good fit or not, and make an informed decision to engage or disengage based on data.

## 2) TRIGGER EVENT

It had been two weeks since Steve introduced the customer fit concept to his team. There was very little pushback. Even the veterans adopted the tool, saying it was intuitive and easy to use. However, many also commented, "I do this now."

The biggest challenge was getting the team, especially the veteran salespeople, to accept that no was often the right answer. They had all been taught: Win every sale! Don't take no for an answer! Never give up! A no means you're closer to a yes. The reality was that if we're *not* systematically—and intentionally—getting a no, we're not doing our jobs effectively. No one argued with the benefit of getting a no, but it always had been based on gut feelings, not hard data such as the fit concept.

Helping to build the rowing shell in exchange for a sales checklist was their agreement, and Steve was back in Wally's workshop sharing the latest update with him. The evening was split between sales and craftsmanship conversations. Wally seemed to go on forever preaching about the unique attributes of mahogany, white oak, cedar, and birch. The reverence with which Wally talked about wood amazed Steve; he'd never given it a second thought.

After a while, Wally ended his soliloquy and asked Steve what feedback he'd been receiving.

"Many of the veterans said that this isn't anything new," said Steve.

"Do you think when a pilot is using a preflight checklist that they come across anything new? I hope not! A checklist empowers people to have a higher baseline of performance by minimizing avoidable failures. I'm sure your veteran salespeople understand the concept of fit and that they should use it, but you told me that overall your team fired about one out of five of your active pursuits based on the fit concept. That's exactly the outcome we want from your checklist!"

"I agree. That's exactly what I was thinking when I heard this!"

"Tell me, Steve, what has to happen before you turn someone into a customer?" asked Wally.

"Well, most of them ask us to provide a quote. The reason could vary. They could have a project coming up, or they're quoting one of their customer's jobs, so they pull together their suppliers. If someone asks us for a quote, we'll usually provide it. The more quotes we put out, the more we close."

Wally gave Steve a look of disappointment. "When you were a salesperson, did all of your customers come from people requesting a quote or proposal? Did you wait for the phone to ring, reverse cold calling, to be successful?"

"No, many of my best customers were the ones I had an opportunity to meet with, perform some discovery, and help identify an area where they could increase their sales, increase productivity, or decrease costs."

"I think you just answered what comes next on the checklist. Why do you think you were more effective in those sales situations?"

"Working together with the decision influencers, I could help them identify a reason to change from the status quo. If there was no reason to change, there wasn't going to be a sale. And because of this, it was easier to get my solution specified in their total project. When I didn't help them identify a problem or a reason for change, I typically ended up being the third or fourth quote. Sometimes I would win, sometimes I'd lose, but it became much more difficult to move forward. I was often commoditized and had to resort to severe discounting to have a chance to win."

"Do you believe you were being disruptive during those conversations?"

"In a way, yes, but I didn't think of it as being disruptive, I was looking for ways to provide them value and solutions to problems, even if they were not aware that they had them. I provided them with a reason to make a change. A reason to make a buying decision. I guess it was more of a consultative approach."

"Do you ask your sales team what's causing the customer to want to make a buying decision?"

"No, I don't always ask, but I believe it could help if I was more consistent. What's causing someone to make a buying decision is critical to uncover. Nobody knows what success looks like without first knowing the problem we're solving. Frankly, that explains why we often lead with our products before we even know the problem. We sell a technical product and talking specs is what our buyers are used to and where we tend to be the most comfortable."

"I think what you're telling me is, once you know the customer is a good fit for you based on your criteria, you cannot bring them value until you understand the problem they're trying to solve, the trigger event, if you will. And if they don't see a trigger event, you need to create one with them," said Wally.

"I agree. Make sure that they are a fit and then determine why they are buying—what is the problem that they are trying to solve. It flows! I need to coach my team into exploring the reason for change," said Steve with excitement. "I like the term *trigger event*. It's simple and catchy!"

"What do you suppose the impact is on each sale if you don't know or don't develop a trigger event?" asked Wally.

Steve knew he had a veteran sales team. They had a habit of breezing past this area of a sales conversation, avoiding it, or talking about the science behind their solution more than selling. He reflected back on the joint calls he made with Juanita and how he could have helped her identify a trigger event at Twin Manufacturing with the QC manager. That would have had a dramatic impact on her ability to move the conversation forward and better tailor the solution. He sees that he now needs to have this conversation on every pursuit.

"We can't maximize the value we bring to our customer and we're very vulnerable to the competition if we don't have a trigger event. Our message becomes all about us, and all we do is talk about our machines instead of those who are most impacted. We start developing a solution without really knowing the full problem we're trying to solve."

"Let me ask you one more question, Steve. What impact does the source of the trigger event have on your ability to profitably close the order?"

"I'm not sure what you mean by source, Wally."

"Well, I believe trigger events can come from three sources. First, the customer can uncover or identify the trigger event. Second, you said that you often can uncover a trigger event. And third, if you can do this, I assume your competition can too. Agree?"

"Yes, I hadn't looked at it that way."

"What's the impact if you're quoting a project where your competition developed the trigger event?"

"Not good. At that point we tend to take a 'me too' approach—we can match what they're proposing. But unless we have a very compelling reason, it's a losing battle."

"So, we agree. For every quote, you need to know the trigger event."

"Absolutely. I'm going to write that down below Fit," said Steve as he grabbed the pencil and walked toward the blueprint where the checklist was being developed.

Over the next few weeks, Steve was busy ensuring his team engaged customers that were a good fit and worked to identify or create a trigger event.

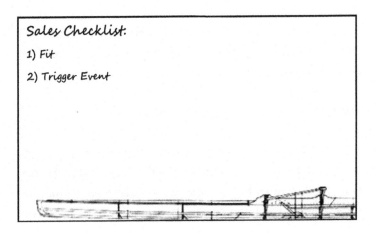

Joe saw measurable changes quickly in both the sales numbers and Steve's confidence. Weekly sales meetings were focused, the dialog had shifted to fit and trigger events, no longer just about delivery issues, pricing issues, new competitors, the Vikings' last loss, and so forth. Joe was now actively participating in the meetings, as he had the checklist and confidently knew exactly what to ask. His increased visibility to the sales opportunities allowed him to better allocate resources where they would produce the maximum return. He was actually beginning to look forward to sales meetings.

The sales team was somewhat surprised with Joe's willingness to invest in the opportunities that were a good fit and where they clearly understood the trigger event. Joe even offered ideas on how to bring more value to the customer than the salespeople had thought of doing.

Joe requested a meeting with Steve to review the sales forecast. "Steve, great sales meeting this morning. It was refreshing to see the regional managers coaching each other on the fit criteria instead of talking about their own worlds. It was interesting to see them change from a yes to a no and easily identify what to work on next. This is great stuff!"

*In seven years, I've never seen Joe this excited about sales,* thought Steve as he sat across the desk from him. *Joe has been through sales training before—he was at our event two years ago, although he didn't sit through most of it, but he's never involved himself in sales conversations until now.*

Joe continued, "From my understanding, we want to focus on customers in our sweet spot, those that have a good fit. And our customers must have a trigger event, or else they will never make a buying decision. And if we don't understand the trigger event, we cannot develop the optimum solution. In the past, we would just take them through our fifty-seven-page PowerPoint presentation of why they should choose NST and by the end of the presentation, we would wonder why everyone was looking at their phone."

Joe chuckled as he pulled a notebook out of his shelf that contained a copy of their company slide deck entitled NST: World Class Solutions. Joe saw slide after slide of NST: World Class Service & Support, Industry Leading Technology, We Believe in Customer Partnerships, and on and on. Just then, Joe had an "aha" moment. *Who wouldn't say they are world class, industry leading, and all this other stuff?! This doesn't differentiate us. I bet our customers have to sit through three or four of these presentations, and the only thing that is different are the logos! There is nothing about how we are uniquely positioned to solve their trigger event. Ouch!*

This was what Steve was working for, things were clicking. Their meeting wrapped up, and Steve passed the second-floor offices on the way back to the stairs. Juanita got Steve's attention just as he put his hand on the door.

"Steve, do you have a minute? I need your coaching." Somewhat sheepishly, she said, "I lost the Apollo order this week... I had forecasted it as a win, and I didn't get it. It was a surprise."

This was the first major sales pursuit that didn't go as planned under Steve's watch. *I knew exactly which one she's talking about,* he thought. He was blindsided. There were plenty of significant, active pursuits out, but this was big. Joe had been watching this one. They sat down in Steve's office.

"Okay, Juanita, let's break this one down. Tell me specifically how they scored on our customer fit criteria."

"It was a big order. They would have been a great customer for us. I've met with them a handful of times over the last nine months. But I think they went with our competitor who beat us on price—"

Steve interrupted, "How much lower were they?"

"From what I could tell, about 8%."

"But what about our shorter delivery time? And our support?" Suddenly Steve caught himself. He'd fallen into the trap of not using what he knew he should—the checklist. He suddenly felt much calmer and in control as he knew how to systematically, and nonemotionally, analyze the outcome based on data and not get lost in all the static.

"Wait a minute, let's back up. Tell me again the criteria we use to define fit," asked Steve.

Juanita read right off the Customer Fit card that Steve had created for the team. "Well, first we look for companies that appreciate our brand and value. Second, we look for key people that are accessible. Third, our contacts must be engaged. Fourth, open and honest. And finally, they must meet a certain deal size."

"Okay, how did they score on those five criteria? Which of the criteria were a yes and which were a no? Think back to all of your conversations and the information you discovered."

"Purchasing said that they loved us, and that we shouldn't talk to anyone else in the company as it was their decision. They kept telling me that we were looking great, just keep sharpening my pencil. But at the end, they said our price was too high and they were going with our competitor—"

"I'm sorry, Juanita, they 'loved' us? I don't think that's one of our criteria. Correct me if I'm wrong, but what I'm hearing is that you were stuck with purchasing, other key people were not accessible to you, they weren't open and honest with their communication, they didn't appreciate your value-added services and brand, and finally, all contacts were not engaged. Is that accurate?" said Steve.

Juanita slowly looked through each point. "Yes, you're right, but—"

Steve cut her off, "Juanita, remember, success is getting an accurate yes or no. There are no maybes! Top-performing salespeople excel at getting one or the other."

"Okay, so that's a score of one out of five. They only met the size criterion. What could I do differently next time?"

"First, great job identifying and scoring it as a one. We want to make this as binary as possible and put trust into the criteria we have. Having one out of five is great! That may sound backward, but we need to have it right. We can't coach if we're not accurate. We need to focus our time and resources on opportunities we're more likely to win. Next time, read the criteria out loud and ask yourself if and why they deserve a yes as you're moving along. We don't want a yes for the sake of getting a yes. That will just get us blindsided. Our goal is to get an accurate answer. I think I've mentioned this to you before, but when pilots are going through their checklist and they identify a problem, have they failed? Of course not, they're just doing their jobs. The same applies to us. As professional salespeople, we can also have a checklist, and getting a no in that checklist doesn't mean we've failed."

Juanita showed signs of relief. She was nervous about this conversation, as most salespeople would be. She was emotionally invested in the pursuit and had used a tremendous amount company resources to see this sale go forward. She also feared the consequences if it didn't, sales conversations were not dealt with like this in the past.

"Juanita, I'm not sure if you know this, but our sales team loses about three out of every four opportunities. This means what we've been doing doesn't work most of the time. So, if you can identify some of those losses earlier and make an informed decision to disengage, you're on your way to becoming salesperson of the year...or the next VP of sales!" said Steve.

Juanita smiled sheepishly. "Come on now, I was only kidding about being future VP of sales. But thanks, Steve, for all this information and support."

"Well, I'm glad you find all this helpful. One more point, Juanita, there may be times we pursue a customer that isn't a good fit for us, but there needs to be a compelling reason to do so. We need to go into pursuits like that with our eyes open and try to minimize our vulnerability."

Steve could see Juanita soaking it all in, and he found it very gratifying.

"Let's take this a step further. I saw Gopher Manufacturing is moving forward with us. Great job! Tell me about that sale!"

"Well, they score a five on our customer fit criteria. They asked us to quote and I pressed discovery further. I found out that the shop floor had been using older machines that wouldn't hold the increased tolerances their customer demanded. In addition, the labor component was making them uncompetitive."

"Did you quote one of our machines?" asked Steve.

"I did, but that wasn't going to solve the real problem they had. They didn't just have a problem holding the tolerances—most of our competitors could address that. They also needed assistance taking the work and getting it up and running on the new equipment. They downsized a few years ago and didn't have the staff to do this internally. But Joe said, based on the fit and trigger event, he's willing to invest some of our internal engineering resources."

Steve was ecstatic. He thought, *Just as it should, the checklist was working without me having to micromanage it! This can scale! On top of that, Joe was involved!*

"That's perfect, Juanita! See, once you validate a fit and identify the trigger event, or events, and solve them with our customer, our chances for a profitable sale significantly increase. It's important to keep peeling the onion back. They want a new machine. Why? What's the problem they're trying to solve? It usually takes multiple questions to uncover the true trigger event; often, our customers don't understand this. Picture yourself peeling back that onion, one layer at a time. They may not see the bigger picture, or they only see what's important to their specific role. We have to help them understand the root cause and solve it. If we don't uncover the trigger event, we end up leading with our products and commoditizing ourselves."

Steve started to think more about trigger events. He had an inkling of what Wally might bring up next: Did you win all of the pursuits where you either solved a trigger event or developed one? Steve knew the answer was no. Actually, some of his most expensive, resource-intensive lost sales, or "science projects" as

Joe liked to call them, never purchased. He knew there must be more to the checklist.

## 3) SALES TARGET

Steve's meeting with Juanita wrapped up fifteen minutes before his weekly regional manager conference call. Five managers and Steve got together for an hour to review the pipeline. This was a carryover from Steve's predecessor. However, it became apparent to Steve that the discussion was focused on product issues, delivery issues, requests for more engineering time, logistics, and various complaints or problems. There was very little "strategic" sales talk, it was "busy" talk. In Steve's eyes, this was the static that kept him from hearing where the salespeople were actually positioned with opportunities. Steve realized that he needed to change this dynamic. Yes, the "busy" conversations were important, but in reality, they had little to do with the next steps to move sales forward, or to potentially disengage if it wasn't likely they would win.

Steve could barely hear two attendees who were calling from their cars. *There must be a better way to do this*, Steve thought. The call seemed so distracted, moving from one topic to the next without any real agreement on the next steps.

*Anything new in your territory? I see the Vikings lost again... How can we better help you and your team? What can we do to close some orders? What customer news do you have?*

The conversation did not define a specific plan, accountability was nonexistent. Steve believed that his team wasn't purposely avoiding accountability, they just didn't know how to systematically identify next steps and those who would be responsible. They all worked hard and wanted to do the right thing—they just didn't know what the right thing was. Steve viewed this as an opportunity and not a problem.

A few managers were still trying to stomach that Joe had selected Steve, this was a unique challenge that internally promoted leaders often faced.

Steve picked Bob, the West territory manager, to start the roundtable discussion. "Bob, how's the West doing? Tell me about your priority sales pursuits and let's coach each other using the new mini checklist." There was a slight pause. *Let's see how strategic we can keep this,* Steve thought as he doodled on his notepad:

## Be Strategic, Not Busy!

Bob began, "Hi, Steve and team, the West is sunny as usual. Our top pursuit is with Motion Alliance. They're a 'big fish' for us out here and we're bidding on their most recent project. Louie is our sales engineer. Fortunately, I know one of their engineers really well. I've worked with him for years. They're going to need six of our 300M horizontal machining centers, plus pallet changers—by the way, our last order of 300Ms was delivered with the wrong tool holders. Did anyone else have that issue?" Bob doesn't give time for a response before continuing, "Steve, can we get an engineer on our future calls here? I tell ya', I'm constantly having to deal with service and delivery requests and I think we should talk through it. It's fortunate that my customers trust me."

Nancy, the East manager was quick to respond, "Our latest order of 300Ms was six weeks ago and we had the same issue. I'm also finding that the installation specs need to be talked through with the machine rigger."

Steve bristled. *What is happening and where is this conversation heading?* Steve was about to end the call early due to frustration. This was no longer a "sales meeting", this was an operations and engineering meeting. The team was following the path of least resistance, talking about everything but selling.

Steve thought, *I'm asking for everyone to talk specifically about their sale, but everyone has their own ideas of what that means. We don't have a consistent, systematic way of discussing our sales opportunities. This has to be part of our problem.*

Steve interjected, "Time out here!" There was a short silence. "We're way off track. Bob, let's talk about the tooling issue later. This is a sales meeting where we talk about selling. I understand that everything you shared is important, and I'm going to help you solve it, but during this hour we need to coach each other on moving sales forward, nothing else. Agree?"

Steve felt like he was herding cats. Being direct and forward was exhausting, especially when you were creating buy-in to a new culture. But enough was enough, sales meetings were supposed to be for discussing sales.

"So, let's start again. Bob, using the checklist, is there a customer fit?"

Bob was quick to respond, "Well, actually, right now, no. But we have three out of five on fit, two of them being question marks. We know they need the 300Ms and want to close them in two weeks."

*Now that's something we can coach to!* thought Steve. "Great, three out of five. Has Louie identified a trigger event or reason for change?"

"Not fully, it's still a question mark until we can find the source of the problem they're trying to solve. We were quick to respond to the request for proposal, but we all know that an RFP isn't a trigger event," said Bob.

"Regarding the date, you said two weeks. Is that when you want to close them or when they want to make a buying decision?" asked Steve.

"What's the difference?" said Bob.

"Well, we want to close them by a certain time—a salesperson always wants to keep the sale moving forward, but what happens if we don't know when they want to make a buying decision?" Steve thought further how to best describe the difference. "Think of it this way, how are we impacted if we don't know what they want to buy, how much, and the date when they want to make a decision? What would that do to our inventory or our production forecast? We need to be asking these questions earlier before getting blindsided. We have to have a target to aim for in the sale."

There was silence on the call, a first. Steve thought, *How do I coach Bob? How do I get Bob to coach Louie the same way that I would? He did a good job at identifying he wasn't sure of the trigger event.*

Then the coaching became obvious to Steve. "Bob, great job identifying that Louie isn't sure of the trigger event—that's a best practice in selling! Now, when you coach Louie later today, what's that going to look like?"

Bob sounded confused, knowing that more was being expected of him. "Well, I'd let him know we can address the issues with the tooling and delivery—"

Steve cut him off, "That's a topic for another conversation. How are you going to coach him from strictly a selling perspective?"

"Oh, that's easy, I'm going to talk to him about how he's going to identify the trigger event when he has his next call. I'll ask him whom he is going to ask, how he's going to explain why it's important, and then have him role-play with me how he's going to ask. Louie is so technical, sometimes he glosses over the selling portion."

"Bob, that's wonderful! Great coaching! Hopefully, given the same situation, he will coach it the same way."

"Okay, Bob, we're not done yet!"

Steve could almost see the you-have-to-be-kidding-me look on Bob's face. "When you meet with Louie next week, what will your coaching be?"

"I'll see where he is on his other pursuits and how he's doing relative to the checklist."

"That's true, that's a good answer, but what's your coaching relative to Motion Alliance?"

"Oh, I see where you're going. I'm going to ask about the trigger event."

Steve quickly responded, "Perfect! Yes! Going forward, our coaching will always go back to the checklist with the goal of getting a yes or a no to each item. Either is a win for us. This way, we're all going to be coaching exactly the same way and our sales engineers are going to be selling the same way—no variation! Think how much easier our jobs will be!"

Proud of Bob, and himself, Steve sat back and could see there was buy-in. He then stared at the mini checklist in front of him, reflecting on his coaching. The next step became obvious. Once they knew the customer fit and trigger event, they had to have some type of target. *Sales target!* he thought. *We need to know what we're selling, how much, and when to make sure we can deliver.*

"Remember, everyone, when you're coaching your team on each sale, we're investing resources to move it forward—from visiting the customer, engineering support, marketing support, working on the proposal, and finally delivering the proposal. It's important for us to understand how pursuing marginal accounts negatively impacts our numbers and performance. We need to review our sales opportunities more from the viewpoint of an engineer: It's just data—the more accurate the data, the better the decision making."

## 4) DECISION-MAKING PROCESS

It was a beautiful June day—sunny and 72 degrees. Steve was gaining confidence in his role. A couple of days after his own "aha" sales target moment while coaching his regional managers, Steve visited Wally and found him sorting through pieces of wood. Steve shared that the customer fit and the trigger event were working great for his team. He updated the checklist on the blueprint with the third criterion—sales target.

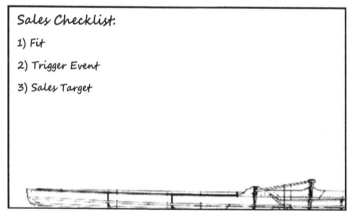

"We just lost a major order that Joe was watching closely," said Steve.

"What happened on this one?" asked Wally.

"Are you saying I should practice what I preach? Good catch. It turned out that the buyers we were talking to ultimately took the recommendation to the vice president of manufacturing. Basing on what the buyers had told us, we thought we had it won, we really did. They loved our solution, it was a good fit for us, we knew what was causing them to buy, and we knew exactly what they were buying," Steve responded.

Thinking for a moment, Steve added, "I know we have a tendency to provide free consulting to customers, especially when it's a new machine for us—we're all machine tool geeks and want to see the latest and greatest machines in action."

"But you still lost. Any idea why?" Wally asked.

"Well, yes, the VP reviewed the project and didn't approve the budget. Total surprise."

Wally continued to examine a piece of 4-mm mahogany that he was considering using, pondering if the knot in the middle of the piece would be a problem. Wally said, almost in passing, "Is this something that your team knows to do, but just missed it on this sale?"

"Oh, definitely. We talk about it, we just sometimes forget," Steve responded.

"Let me ask you this, Steve," said Wally while he was adjusting the block plane with the precision of a jeweler. "What would you have done differently if you had known that the VP of manufacturing had to review and sign off on the project?"

"I'm sure we would have tried to meet with him and find out

about how they were going to make the buying decision, and, in hindsight, if the project was funded. Also, I know we could have helped them come up with a more substantial ROI calculation. There are cost savings that we know weren't included in their analysis that should have been."

"Steve, would you hand me that rasp on the bench?" Wally asked. "How are you going to make sure this doesn't happen again?"

Steve responded immediately, "I'm going to put it on our checklist!"

"So, what you're telling me is, going forward, your salespeople need to find out what the decision-making process is and if the project is funded. If you looked at all your other key sales opportunities, how many of those had a salesperson who knew what the decision-making process was and verified that it wasn't a 'science project,' as you call it?" asked Wally.

"Ouch!" responded Steve. "Taking that a step further, I know we have active, forecasted, critical pursuits out there right now where we don't fully understand the decision-making process."

Wally handed Steve a pencil and nodded toward the checklist on the blueprint. Steve added to the checklist: "Decision-Making Process."

"Let me ask you another question, Steve: Were they a fit?" Wally asked, pointing to the fit criteria on the blueprint.

"Yes, I think so."

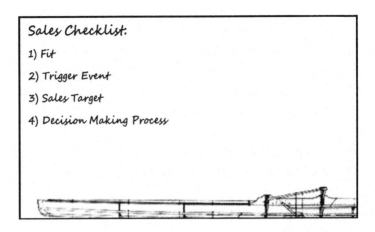

"Walk me through the criteria, Steve."

"Well, they did appreciate our brand and value. Price was not an issue with them. They were not the lowest-cost producer, and they valued our quality and support. They were willing to pay a premium for it. At first, I thought they were accessible, but in reality, they weren't, at least not for this project, so that's a no. I think I just answered the next one—they weren't engaged. They did have open and honest communication; we just neglected to ask the right questions. And the deal was for $250k, so we were okay there. So, they scored a three out of five, which is the minimum to move forward."

"Nice job, and don't be defensive. This is just data—it's not good, it's not bad, it just is. It's just like engineering, Steve—the better the data, the better the decision making. Knowing what you now know, how would you have coached your salesperson?"

"I would have gone through the checklist item by item, including what we just discussed. I wouldn't have taken anything for granted. Or just assumed that because one of the items was a yes during the last meeting that it may now be a no. That would have uncovered what we missed—the vice president wasn't accessible or engaged on this pursuit. The fact that he might have been in the past didn't matter for this pursuit. I guess that's why pilots go through a checklist every time they fly. They know that each flight is different, even if they're flying the same airplane on a new flight later in the day. I had looked at the checklist as something of a one-and-done kind of a thing—once we checked something off, it was done. But now I can see with how long and complex our sales are that items very well can change over the sales cycle."

"What would that have done?"

"Simple, Wally, we would have found out much earlier that there was an issue with this pursuit, and we could either have addressed it or made the decision to stop the pursuit, or at least minimized the resources we were throwing at it."

"That's great, Steve! Feels good to be getting control, doesn't it?"

"Yes, it really does. I've noticed the same thing with my managers and sales engineers. As a group, we're not so defensive when we get a no, we don't feel like we failed. Actually, we feel as though we're doing our jobs correctly."

"Steve, what are your thoughts on what you have so far on your checklist that will help you accomplish your three objectives?" asked Wally.

"Well, I can see all of this helping with each of the objectives. We're already experiencing much less variability in how we sell and coach," Steve said. "We're disengaging from customers more than we ever have before, which will reduce our loss rate, our defects. And we're much more focused on where we invest our engineering time and company resources, so our waste is being reduced," explained Steve with a smile slowly growing on his face as if to say, *Yes! I can do this!*

"That's great, Steve. I agree, you're making solid progress."

"Solid progress?" Steve replied. "I think we have our checklist, I'm accomplishing all of Joe's objectives."

"Okay, we'll see, just keep an open mind."

## 5) DECISION INFLUENCERS

Steve was preparing for a meeting with the Midwest regional sales manager, Chris, and two local salespeople, Juanita and Tom. The four of them sat down in the conference room overlooking the Mississippi River.

*Minneapolis skyline & the Mississippi River*

Chris had been with NST for twenty years, five in a management role. He had a background in engineering and was initially hired to manage the technical product training curriculum. Boredom struck, and he continued to bring a high value to sales-related conversations. So when a territory sales rep position opened, he decided to make the move. As a veteran, many of the salespeople would follow his lead. He had a reputation for always having "better" ways of doing things. His behavior wasn't disruptive, but often was not supportive. It was apparent to Steve that Chris felt he should have received the promotion, not Steve. Steve realized, however, that gaining Chris's support would be critical to his success.

Tom was the most veteran salesperson, nearing his twenty-fourth anniversary. He was quiet, somewhat reserved, and enjoyed the technical nature of NST's products. His customers appreciated his ability to talk specifications and share what was new from NST and his openness to provide free consulting. Tom was a middle-of-the-pack sales performer but was consistent and reliable.

"Steve, we're struggling with a major pursuit. They don't want to pay our price, so we're going to need to offer a discount," explained Chris. Steve nodded, encouraging Chris to continue with more details as he pulled out his sales checklist with four items on it.

Chris continued, "They're a pump manufacturer. We've done work in the past and, unfortunately, one of the machines we sold them has a number of service problems. Plus, we had some delays getting parts in to fix it. It's an interesting pump they're manufacturing. It's going to be machined out of 2205 stainless steel so that it can withstand the chemicals used in a paper-processing plant. The application is really cutting edge. The new pump is about half the size but has the same performance specifications. My key contact was an engineer, but he's gone now."

Steve, trying to hide his frustration, held up his hands in the shape of a T. "Time out. You're talking about everything except the sales checklist." Steve thought, *This is exactly why our sales meetings drag on and on and never accomplish much of anything.*

"Chris, using the checklist I gave you, tell me how you're positioned."

There was a brief silence. Chris and Tom opened their portfolios and pulled out their laminated cards. Juanita already had hers on top of her portfolio. Holding his team accountable was getting easier for Steve. It was time to start seeing measurable change.

Chris, feeling sheepish after rambling on and on, looked at the beginning of the checklist. "They're a good fit—we've done business with them before. The trigger event is that the new pump needs to be in production in six months so they can make their customer's deadline. They will need new machine tools in three months to do so. We have verified the decision-making process and that the project is funded. That's what we know so far."

"Okay, interesting. Let's talk a little more about their fit. They may have been a fit before, but we all know how quickly things change. Are they a good fit today?"

"Well, I think so," Chris responded.

"Okay, let's review this systematically, using our checklist. What have you observed recently that makes you feel they appreciate our brand and value?"

"Hmm, well, they used to, and I don't think that has changed."

"So, what you're telling me is that for this sale, you don't know if they appreciate our brand and value?"

"That's fair," Chris said. Tom, avoiding eye contact, stared at his checklist.

"Great, all we want is accurate data. Everything else will take care of itself."

"Okay, that makes sense. It's just hard when we think success is a yes answer and failure is a no answer. Frankly, it's easier just being accurate... I don't feel I have to defend my answers!"

The rest of the sales team laughed—a laugh of relief, the kind that often happens during tense meetings.

Steve continued, "Now, with that in mind, walk us through the rest of the fit criteria."

"Okay, well, I don't know yet if they currently appreciate our value. Historically, they have never been a price buyer. I think this is still the case, but frankly, I don't know. I do know that the key decision influencers have not yet been accessible on this project. They certainly are not engaged yet. And, well, I don't know yet if they are going to be open and honest. But they meet the size criteria! Ultimately, I believe they will be a good fit, but I'm not sure yet."

"Great job, Chris! Based on this, what are you going to do?"

"That's easy! I'm going to make it a priority for us to find out if they are a fit or not before we invest a lot more time on them."

"Let's continue on the checklist. Do we know the trigger event? What caused the decision to put a new pump into production? What are they trying to accomplish?" asked Steve.

"I know the application, but purchasing isn't able to answer the questions that I have, it's too technical for them. But they're saying it's their decision and not to go around them," said Chris.

"In my experience, anytime someone says, 'Don't go around me,' I picture a cartoon bubble above their head that says, 'This is *not* my decision!' So, how do the other people who could impact the decision feel about your value?" asked Steve.

"We know there are other people involved in the project since it's a new line for them. But our conversations have stayed with one contact," said Chris.

"So, I think what you're telling me is, you're stuck with purchasing and there may be other decision influencers involved. Is that fair to say?" asked Steve.

THE SALES CHECKLIST™

*"This is my decision, don't go around me!"*

"Yes, that's fair," Chris responded slightly defensively.

"How often are we successful when we only sell to purchasing? What are your chances of winning the business?" asked Steve.

The team sat silently for a second. Juanita replied, "Not good."

"I agree. If we're able to identify and meet with all the people on the project and discuss our solution, would the probability of winning increase?" asked Steve.

"Absolutely!" said Chris. Steve then turned to Tom and asked, "So, who else can potentially impact this decision?"

"Well, not in any particular order, design engineers, machine operators, quality control, finance, maintenance, and probably the VP of manufacturing."

"So, is it fair to say that the risk of going around purchasing is less than the risk if you don't?" asked Steve.

"Yes," said Tom.

"Based on that, where should we go next according to the checklist?" said Steve.

"It's actually pretty simple, after reviewing it, I'd need to identify all the people who can influence the buying process," said Tom.

"Okay, that's a measurable outcome for you, Tom, identify and engage with the others who can influence the sale. What are your thoughts on how you would do that?"

"Gee, that's tough, Steve. I know purchasing won't tell me."

"That's okay, Tom, we're just talking about data here. Have you sold equipment to them before?"

"Oh yah! About three years ago, I sold them two five-axis robots for a sealant application."

"Great! Could any of those contacts answer the question for you?" asked Steve.

"I suppose. They're not involved with this project, but I'm sure they know what's going on."

"Tom, I think you just identified your next step: Connect with a couple of your previous contacts and ask them if they could give you a little guidance. Do you think they would do that?"

"Yeah, I do. We worked very closely to get the sealant cell up and running. They really appreciated the extra support I gave them. That's a good idea!"

"Moving on, let's take a critical sale that you've won. Do you have one in mind?" Steve asked Juanita and Chris.

"Um, yes, we can use Northstar Fabricators," said Juanita. "Hmmm, where to start..." she said as she thought back to six months ago.

Steve interrupted, "Trust the checklist. What's the first area we focus on?"

"Oops, good point, sorry. Regarding customer fit, they were a four out of five, so yes to fit. The trigger event was that they were having ongoing quality issues with their previous supplier that was causing them to miss key deliveries and we knew what they were buying. We knew the decision-making process and identified that it wasn't going to be budgeted until a certain date," explained Juanita.

"Wonderful! The fact you identified it wasn't funded shows that you're using the checklist perfectly. Knowing that it's not funded, we won't get blindsided," explained Steve. "Tell me more about the people involved in making the decision," he continued.

"There was the design engineer, who developed the specifications that we had to meet or exceed. He reported to the VP of manufacturing, who was concerned about how we would impact his production. I think that's it." Juanita paused briefly.

Steve was seeing the power of the checklist. Salespeople tended to lull themselves into skipping steps, even when they knew they were important. The checklist was helping Juanita get it right.

"No, wait," she continued. "There was one more person who became involved—their CFO. There were parts of our solution that were unique, and she became involved to quantify the overall ROI. So, the engineer wrote the initial specifications and narrowed the number of companies that could quote from five to three. The VP of manufacturing met with all three, but I think the most time was spent with us. The CFO ultimately pulled the trigger."

"So, when you're successful, you're identifying and engaging with the key decision influencers who can influence the outcome. I think the three of us are in the next item of our sales checklist: Identify and engage all the people involved in the sale, the decision influencers."

The meeting lasted another ten minutes, and Chris began to take a slightly more active role in coaching Juanita and Tom.

Steve began to reflect on the meeting. It started out in chaos. No wonder previous sales meetings failed to produce actionable outcomes. No wonder Joe got so frustrated! But this meeting later on became quite productive.

Steve was jolted back to reality. "Steve... Steve, anything else you wanted to discuss today?" asked Chris.

"No...no, good job. Thank you."

## 6) MENTOR

As the three of them began to get up from the table, Juanita pulled out her latest call notes from a meeting with Sam Johnson, a manufacturing engineer of Hess Manufacturing. "Steve, can we talk about one more account?"

"Of course," Steve said as they sat back down. Steve was anxious to hear an update but also very interested to continue to observe Chris's ability and desire to coach his field reps. A major concern for Steve was how his managers coached. He'd been working diligently on how to coach the checklist, It's just data, yes and no are both right answers, systematically disengaging from opportunities is something top performers do consistently, and so forth.

"I haven't made much progress on this new project, I mean sales target. This one is double the size of any project I've been involved with before," said Juanita.

Steve waited for Chris to jump in, but when it became apparent that he wasn't going to, he went back to the sales checklist, pointed to the top, and said, "Well, let's start at the beginning."

"Yes! That makes sense, but frankly, it just seems too simple to actually work," said Juanita.

Steve responded only somewhat jokingly, "Juanita, you're right! If it wasn't, you guys wouldn't use it!" Juanita, Chris, and Tom looked at each other and chuckled in agreement.

"Well, my contact has been keeping me updated with news of the project, but based on our conversations regarding decision influencers ten minutes ago, I realized it's time we meet with the other people involved. That will help me understand what's important to each of them and how they will ultimately make their decision."

"I remember meeting Sam at Hess. Do you think he could be my internal advocate, or cheerleader? Could he be someone that drives consensus and sells internally for me?" asked Juanita.

Steve knew that Juanita was in the ballpark but was missing some critical elements. He wanted to encourage Juanita's engagement, but he also knew that he needed to subtly direct the conversation. For far too long he'd seen salespeople relying on a "cheerleader" or "consensus driver" within the prospect company. This had been acting like a crutch because no one could sell their value and solutions better than they could. He thought for a moment before saying, "I think you're onto something here, Juanita. Let's expand on this."

"When I think back on our most important wins and losses, there was a common thread. When we won, we tended to have someone who would guide us. Conversely, when we lost, more often than not, we didn't have a person such as this," said Steve.

"Exactly!" said Chris, who was now leaning forward and fully engaged. "I always try to develop a person like this, well at least I know that I should, but frankly sometimes I get too busy. I call this person a mentor as he or she is the person I go to for guidance. I don't want them to sell for me—I'm a better salesperson than my mentors! Also, I've found over the years that if they did try to sell for me, they lost credibility within the company."

Steve was now sitting back in his chair, trying to look like he was just taking it all in, but internally he was yelling to himself, *Yes! Yes! This is perfect! They're engaged and taking ownership of the checklist. I wish Joe was here!*

He was also thinking how ironic it was that Chris, the company skeptic, but well-respected sales leader, was becoming such an advocate of the checklist.

Chris asked Juanita, "What action would we want from Sam in more of a 'mentoring' way based on the information you still need to move the sale forward?"

"Based on the checklist, I need him to introduce me to the other decision influencers. I need to engage with all the people involved, don't I?" asked Juanita.

"Exactly," said Steve and Chris simultaneously. Realizing that his goal was for his managers to become effective coaches, he quickly realized his mistake. Steve quickly said, "I'm sorry, Chris, you've got this." Steve sat back and subtly rested his hand on his jaw to show he wasn't going to interrupt and that he wanted Chris and Juanita to work through the concept of mentor.

Chris continued, "One of the challenges I've had is verifying that someone is really my internal advocate or mentor. Sam introducing you to someone is something he would not do for all competitors. So if he does, that's a good sign; if he doesn't, that's a bad sign. Um, I don't mean bad sign anymore—it's just the checklist working. That's a powerful person to have on your side in a sale. Also, if he doesn't, what does that tell you?"

"That I need to find a mentor in someone else, or there's a possibility they're not a good fit," said Juanita.

"That's exactly right, Juanita. Great job!" said Chris. "Did you want to add anything else, Steve?"

"No, no, you guys nailed it! Oh, Chris, can you stay for a minute? I have one other issue to cover with you," said Steve.

Once they were alone, Steve asked, "Chris, how do you feel about using the checklist to coach your team, going forward?"

"Well, honestly, Steve, you know I've been here a long time, and it's nothing personal, but you're probably the sixth or seventh VP of sales I've worked with. Each came in with their new ideas. The ideas were good, but obviously, nothing stuck. I thought this was the same situation—give it six months and it would be forgotten. You know I have the reputation as the company skeptic, but I like your checklist—it's easy to use. Now, there is nothing new on it, I know all of these things, but I do realize I may skip some steps now and then, and this checklist prevents me from doing that. I have to admit, I'm a better coach now. I now know what to coach, no guessing, and the meetings are so much more focused. You know how they used to drag on and on and on!"

"Thanks for the input, Chris!" said Steve. "By the way, I didn't know you were the company skeptic," Steve said to Chris with a grin.

After dinner that evening, Steve strolled over to Wally's. It was an unusually warm and humid July evening. Steve could see and hear the thunderstorm that was blowing in. He found Wally applying spar varnish to the inside of the shell.

"Hey, Wally! How are you?"

"Great, how are you?"

"I'm well, thanks. Wow, that varnish really makes the wood just glow!"

"It does, doesn't it? Do you want to give it a try? It's very relaxing, or maybe that's just the fumes..."

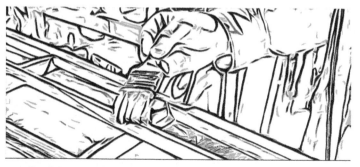

*"Applying varnish is very relaxing...or maybe that's just the fumes."*

"Sure, I'd love to give it a try, Wally."

"Just long, smooth strokes. You'll have to go back and look for drips. This is the first coat of varnish, and to get it to soak into the wood, I thinned it 50% with denatured alcohol."

"Got it. Hey, while we're talking, we added to the sales checklist today. We found that we were vulnerable if we didn't identify and engage all the key people influencing the decision. I'm calling it decision influencers. What do you think?"

"I think you missed a spot by the bulkhead."

"No, about the addition to the checklist?"

"I think it's great, Steve. Here, I'll add it to the list."

"Before you do that, we came up with another one. We identified that when we win, especially a complex sale, that we more often than not have someone who guides us through the sale.

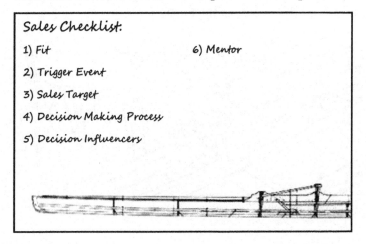

Sales Checklist:
1) Fit
2) Trigger Event
3) Sales Target
4) Decision Making Process
5) Decision Influencers
6) Mentor

The person gives us advice, kind of mentors us. They don't sell for us, but they help us understand the dynamics of a complex sale. We know we should do it, it's not a new concept, we just sometimes forget, so I want to add it to the checklist."

Wally was smiling to himself; Steve had taken ownership of the checklist and was making it complete.

"I think that's a great idea, Steve. What do you want to call it?"

"How about just mentor? It's a person we go to for advice...or learn how to build a boat..."

Wally chuckled and added the two items to the checklist.

## 7) TRIGGER PRIORITY

It was finally Friday evening and Steve stopped by Wally's house after getting home from the office. Steve saw that Wally wasn't there and decided to take Sally out for dinner. Wally had been talking about this great restaurant—The Chanhassen Curling Club—and Steve suggested to Sally that they try it. Sally gave Steve "the look," the no-seriously-you're-taking-me-to-a-curling-club-for-dinner? look.

At the curling club, they saw Wally and Gertie enjoying a couple of drinks. Wally was talking up a storm, and Gertie was content to watch the curling and occasionally nodding in agreement.

"Hey! Wally and Gertie! How are you two tonight?" said Steve. "Sally, I'd like to introduce you to Wally and his wife, Gertie."

*"Dinner at a curling club?...Why not?"*

"Nice to meet both of you. I've heard a lot about you, Wally," said Sally.

"Nice to meet you too, Sally. We're great! Good to see both of you. Please join us. You guys here for dinner, or are you going to throw some rocks? It's a curling club, after all!" said Wally with a smile.

"No, we're here to have dinner, and I guess to watch..." said Sally.

"We just finished our game and played our arch enemies. At the first end, we lost the flip, which seems to be a habit for us, but Gertie put her first rock six feet short on the line—"

Gertie interrupted, "Wally! We don't need to go through the entire game. Let's eat! Steve and Sally, have you had the beer-battered walleye here? It's wonderful! The tater tot hot dish is on special tonight. It's the best in town! They also have a green bean hot dish that is out of this world. The bars are the best here too!"

Steve and Sally shot each other a quick look. Tater tot casserole? Green bean hot dish? Bars?

Having observed Steve and Sally's quizzical looks, Wally said, "Maybe I should explain. In Minnesota, everyone does hot dishes. Basically, throw anything you like into a casserole dish, add some cream of mushroom soup, and there you go! Bars are brownies, lemon squares, any desert you make in a pan and cut into, well, little bars. Don't worry, you'll learn!"

Later during dinner, Steve said, "I have to tell you, what we now have on the checklist is fantastic. Fit, trigger event, sales target, and decision-making process are great! The salespeople have embraced it. We're closing more business, and Joe is pleased with our progress."

Steve asked Wally, "If it's okay, could I stop by tomorrow morning so we could talk some more?"

"That would be great, Steve," said Wally.

Gertie and Sally looked at each other, and Gertie said, "Enough shop talk boys!"

The following Saturday morning, Steve grabbed a cup of coffee and headed over to Wally's. "What a great week, Wally. I've been spending most days on coaching calls with my team and using our sales checklist. We haven't been this successful at identifying where we stand and moving sales forward, or disengaging from them, since...well...ever. Our team members are even starting to coach each other. Joe is extremely pleased, and

I told him that's why he promoted me!"

Wally chuckled, and Steve took a deep breath and continued, "I'm here to help with the boat...and because we lost a big sale. We didn't actually lose it—I don't think they ever bought anything. I got the news this week from our team in California that the LaFald project wasn't going through."

"Interesting. Walk me through it," said Wally as he was clamping the white oak shear strips to the mahogany bulkheads.

"LaFald is a company that manufactures equipment for breweries, mostly pumps and valves. We couldn't get the VP of manufacturing to sign off on the order. I'm not sure why."

"Interesting. What are your thoughts?" said Wally.

"I just don't know, Wally," said Steve. "They met the fit criteria. The trigger event was that they wanted to increase the throughput for their craft brewing equipment as their sales revenue has grown considerably for that segment."

"When you have a project of this magnitude, does every decision influencer see it as a priority?" asked Wally. Steve looked puzzled. "Let me share an example. You were attempting to get them to purchase new technology. Would anyone view that change as negative?"

"No, of course not, it's new and better technology," said Steve.

"Really? Would the application engineers have to learn a

new machine? Would the maintenance technicians have to learn something new? Would the service department need to stock new parts and learn how to maintain the machine? Also, wouldn't a VP of manufacturing have lots of priorities on their plate? Is this the only project they are working on? Can these projects all be top priorities?" asked Wally.

"No, but the VP agreed that there was a trigger event," said Steve.

"Someone can acknowledge a trigger event, but there may be more pressing issues. We just tend to look at it from our own perspective, not theirs. Were there possibly other trigger events? Ones that had greater urgency for him. Any thoughts on what it might have been?" said Wally.

"Good question. Come to think of it, my mentor mentioned that they may be acquiring a competing manufacturer."

"Hmm, what do you think that means?" asked Wally as he shuffled around the workbench, clamping the shear strips in place.

"I'm not sure. The VP of manufacturing agreed with the trigger event, but I guess it might not have been their top priority, or maybe the competing manufacturer already had the machine tools to do the job."

"Let's go one layer deeper. You're telling me that the VP had a trigger event, but it wasn't enough of a priority for them to take action at this time. Is that accurate?"

"Yes," replied Steve.

"If a key decision influencer doesn't think the trigger event is a priority, then a buying decision will not be made. The checklist should help you create a priority for them to take action. If it's not a priority, the sale will end up in your 'lost' or 'no decision' category. To summarize, you shared with me there was a trigger event, but not everyone agreed that it was a priority. I guess we should call that criterion trigger priority," said Wally.

Steve walked over and updated the sales checklist.

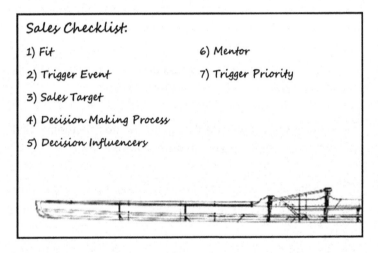

"Steve, if your salesperson doesn't understand or apply the concept of trigger priority, do you feel that he or she is making the same mistake on other key opportunities?"

With a suddenly concerned look on his face, Steve responded, "Yes, I imagine that's right."

"I can see how this will help salespeople coach themselves and help managers coach their teams. In fact, this is exactly what

Joe has been looking for. Now he's able to provide coaching too," said Steve.

"Didn't Joe provide sales coaching before?"

"No, not really. Before we started the checklist, he would come into sales meetings periodically and then usually leave within ten minutes, looking frustrated. He wasn't engaged in sales conversations at all. He'd ask what do we need to do to close a sale, but I don't think he ever felt comfortable coaching to sales. It wasn't like his other department meetings where he felt he could intelligently engage in the discussions.

Before the checklist, he would just ask what's the forecast, what are we going to close, how's the pipeline. Nothing to do with closing more business—just overall numbers. Now he has specific data on every key pursuit. I guess he just feels more empowered that he can help win specific orders, not just ask what do we have to do to meet our numbers."

## 8) ALTERNATIVES

A couple of days later, Steve was back in Wally's garage, admiring the sales checklist.

"Okay, here's another deal I was hoping we could talk about," said Steve. "But first, sometimes when I'm driving home in the evening, I see you sipping on something that certainly isn't a Grain Belt. Can I ask what it is?"

"Of course! Would you like some?" Wally opens the cabinet where he stores his paint, glue, and spar varnish. To the side is a bottle of eighteen-year-old scotch. It was the only container in the cabinet that didn't have any dust on it.

"Yes! Please!" Steve continued, "My top salesperson, Bobby, is pursuing this deal. We've had multiple meetings, and they're a yes for fit." Steve went through each item on the checklist, discussing each quickly and efficiently, not missing a step.

Wally listened while he opened the refrigerator beside his recliner. He pulled out a couple of chilled glasses and added ice into them before also giving an ice cube to Dudley. He poured a couple of fingers of scotch into each glass, and handed one of the glasses to Steve.

"When we first began our sales discussions, you were losing three out of four of your sales pursuits. You had tremendous variation in the execution of your sales team. Managers were not effective at coaching, and it was almost impossible to have an accurate indication of how the salesperson was positioned with the pursuit. How has the checklist impacted your goals?" asked Wally.

"It's had a positive impact on all of that, plus Joe is very pleased. But when Bobby and I discussed his pursuit, we both felt uncomfortable. Something in our gut didn't feel right," said Steve.

"Well, if you two have scored the pursuit correctly, what concerns do you have?" said Wally, taking a sip of scotch.

"Like I said, I can't put our finger on it, it's a gut feeling," said Steve.

"Didn't feel right in your gut? I certainly hope I never get on a flight where the pilots feel something is wrong in their gut but take off anyway. Sounds like maybe the checklist isn't complete, wouldn't you agree?"

Steve replied, "Definitely. I just don't know what's missing."

"I think you do, Steve. Was there anything on the checklist that you didn't do? Not necessarily every time, but at least you were aware of?" asked Wally.

"No, that's one of the aspects that's so appealing to me about the checklist—it provides reminders of only the most critical and important steps, the ones that even top-performing salespeople could miss if they didn't consistently use it. It's helping us to get it right—most of the time."

"Most of the time? Does a pilot's checklist work only most of the time? What are some reasons that your team doesn't close orders these days?" asked Wally.

"The only thing I can think of is they buy from the competition, and we've discussed that sometimes they don't buy anything."

Wally tried sitting comfortably in his recliner next to Dudley, who had tired of the conversation. "Both are true. Last month, you and Sally were looking at either buying a new car or getting your kitchen remodeled."

"I'm not going to forget that," said Steve as he took a sip from his glass and looked at his house through the garage window.

"Judging by the construction at your house, you went with the kitchen over the car, correct?"

"Obviously."

"Why didn't you do both?"

"Frankly, we couldn't afford to do both at the same time."

"So, if I was the salesperson attempting to sell you a car, did I lose the order?"

"Well, no, you didn't lose the order, we just went with the kitchen instead. The car might come later, but we had to prioritize."

"When you say the salesperson didn't lose the order, what do you mean?"

"He didn't lose it. We just didn't buy from him."

"Okay, but the fact is he didn't win the order; he didn't get a commission. The impact is the same whether you bought a competing car, decided to remodel your kitchen, or didn't do anything at all."

"That's fair, Wally."

"So, the car salesperson didn't lose an order to another car salesperson. You had other preferred alternatives for your resources. You simply spent your resources on something else, not even related to a car," said Wally.

"Yes, that's exactly right."

"Let me guess, you told the salesperson, 'Yes, that's the car I want to buy. It's perfect! It's the right color, has the right options, and it's in stock!'"

Steve chuckled. "Were you hiding behind the potted plant is his office? That's almost exactly how the conversation went!"

"Do you think that the salesperson felt like he had the order? Do you think it was forecasted?"

"Yes, I do... I hadn't thought about it that way, Wally."

"If the car salesperson came back to you with a discount, would that have changed what you purchased?" asked Wally.

"No, we still would have gone with the kitchen."

"Back to your sales world, I suspect that your customers have options, or alternatives, beside buying from you. Such as buying from the competition, not buying anything, or using their resources for something else, possibly unrelated. Wouldn't you want to know the alternatives that each key decision influencer is considering?"

Steve paused for a minute and stared at the sales checklist. Reflecting, he said, "Do you realize how many sales pursuits we've spent resources on that didn't move forward because we didn't know what else could have been a priority? We talk about competition all the time, but I wonder how many sales

> **Sales Checklist:**
> 1) Fit
> 2) Trigger Event
> 3) Sales Target
> 4) Decision Making Process
> 5) Decision Influencers
> 6) Mentor
> 7) Trigger Priority
> 8) Alternatives

we've lost, or are currently losing, because they, figuratively, remodeled their kitchen instead of buying a car. Actually, *we were selected,* they just haven't purchased yet."

"I think we just identified another step—I'll add it to the list! All you have to do now is coach Bobby on what he needs to do: Uncover all the individual decision influencer's alternatives and make sure he has strategies to address them. How do you feel about that?" said Wally.

"We just increased our probability of winning, or making the informed decision to disengage," said Steve, as he gave Wally kudos for helping him discover this.

### 9) OUR SOLUTION RANKING

The following week, Steve invited Wally to visit him at the NST office. Wally couldn't help but say yes.

Steve came out to the lobby to greet Wally. "Wally, you didn't have to wear a suit. We're pretty casual here."

"This is business casual to me," said Wally.

On their way through the building, the two stopped by Joe's office, where Steve was much more comfortable now than he was back in November. Joe had written out the eight steps to Steve's checklist on his whiteboard wall. They'd been discussing the criteria each step of the way, along with the top key sales pursuits.

"Wally, I wanted to show you this. Joe has transferred everything we've been discussing onto his whiteboard. Whenever he reviews a pursuit with a salesperson, manager, or me, we go right down the list. We're rarely surprised by losing an order anymore. There are also many pursuits where we make an informed decision to disengage, or at least minimize our resource expenditure. I can provide Joe with fact-based visibility into any sale, and we're eliminating the variation in execution of salespeople and managers. We no longer spend forty-five minutes talking about the entire history of a pursuit. Instead, we spend ten to fifteen minutes and discuss how we're positioned and what we need to do next to move it either forward or out. We've made it a game—anytime someone scores one of the criteria as a no, or changes it from a yes to a no, we celebrate it. We embrace the idea that an accurate score is what we're seeking, not a high score. I want to thank you for all of your help."

"Thanks, Steve, I appreciate that, but I didn't tell you anything you didn't already know. Checklists aren't about reinventing the wheel, they are about making the same wheel *every time*," said Wally.

"It's also had an impact I didn't expect. Now that everyone knows the questions they're going to be asked, it's driving their behavior in front of the customers. And that's ultimately what we want. The team has discovered that not only is the tool simple to use but also that it takes only minutes to ask a decision influencer a couple of questions to change their score. Initially many salespeople thought that it would be difficult to execute the checklist or it would detract from their sales call, but they've learned that it doesn't take much time at all to ask questions such as 'Is this funded?' or 'Who are all the people involved in the buying process?' It literally takes a minute to ask. It's so simple!"

"That's wonderful!" said Wally with a grin as they strolled through the halls of NST.

When they arrived at Steve's office, Steve continued, "But I think we're still missing something, and I have an idea to run by you."

"Sure, you know I'd love to help if I could."

"Thanks, Wally. Well, I understand the concept of alternatives…and I thought, wouldn't it be helpful to know how each individual decision influencer felt about what we're proposing relative to those alternatives?" Steve gestured from the top of the checklist down to the bottom, which was on his office whiteboard, just like in Joe's office.

Wally was distracted by the view of the Mississippi River. The university's rowing team was out training. Steve happened to

catch what Wally was looking at and said, "You know, Wally, there really is a grace to rowing, isn't there? I never noticed that before; it must be a wonderful feeling."

"It certainly is, especially in a wooden rowing shell with a soul, not a plastic Tupperware one," said Wally. He cleared his throat and snapped back into the conversation. "Sorry I got distracted there for a moment, but yes, I think you're really onto something about how the decision influencers feel about your solution relative to all alternatives," confirmed Wally. "We've agreed that some of the decision influencers may have alternatives they're considering. Remember, you are competing against anything that keeps you from getting the check. So, if the key decision influencers decide to do nothing, or to spend the resources on a new computer system rather than what you're selling, you're competing with those in addition to your regular competitors. I agree that it's reasonable that the decision influencers will have their own—and various—ranking systems for their alternatives. You would want to know not only the alternatives being considered by each decision influencer, but also how they rank your solution relative to everything else."

"That makes a lot of sense. I would also want to know what my salesperson is doing to address any situations where we are not the top-ranked alternative."

"What should we call this criterion?"

"How about solution ranking?" said Steve as he writes *9) Solution Ranking* on his whiteboard. "I'll go write this on Joe's board too. We'll see if he notices when he gets back in town," said Steve with a smile.

"I'll make sure to add it on the blueprint."

## 10) INDIVIDUAL IMPACT

It was a Saturday in late July. Wally had recently completed the rowing shell, which was now outside in the sunlight. He'd attached the rigging and sliding seat rowing unit. Steve walked over and looked at the components that he had helped make with a real sense of pride and accomplishment.

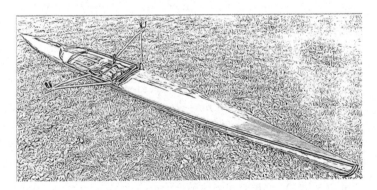

"Beautiful, isn't it? I still can't believe they now make these boats out of plastic, fiberglass, and even carbon fiber. Seems a shame, doesn't it? They don't have any soul," said Wally. Steve couldn't help but agree.

"So, all finished?"

"Almost. I just need to adjust the sliding seat rowing unit," said Wally.

"What a coincidence. We finished the boat at the same time we completed our checklist!" said Steve.

"I'm not sure I know what you mean. The shell isn't quite finished," said Wally.

By now Steve knew what that meant. "Okay, Wally, you're telling me there's more to the checklist, aren't you?"

"Maybe. You tell me," said Wally. "Let me ask you a couple of questions: First, who buys from you?"

"Companies who need machine tools, automation, and tooling."

"Really? How does a 'company' make a buying decision? Name a recent sale you had."

"Alright, we just closed Tower Manufacturing."

"So, Tower Manufacturing signed off on the order?"

"No, it was their vice president of manufacturing, Eileen Eiffel."

"People buy, companies don't. Have you ever received a check signed by a company? I haven't. A person always signs my checks," said Wally with a familiar grin.

"Okay, the company doesn't buy. The people involved in the buying process actually buy."

"Right, so if people are buying, they make buying decisions based on what's in it for them. WIIFM—that means What's In It For Me," said Wally. "Put another way, you and Sally both wanted the kitchen remodeled, didn't you?"

"Yes, we did. Even with all the alternatives, we decided to go with a new kitchen," said Steve.

"How did you choose which company to purchase from?"

"Sally talked with many remodelers but finally chose the one we used because of their design capability and reputation for high-quality work. She thought the way they incorporated a cooking surface into the center island was a nice touch. I liked the company for a different reason: They found a way to inexpensively update our patio. I love to grill and needed more space."

"If I was the remodeling salesperson, would it have been helpful to know that you both wanted a kitchen, but she wanted center island cooking capability and you wanted something totally different—a larger patio for grilling? In essence, what did Sally buy?"

"The kitchen? I don't get it..." said Steve slightly confused and slightly distracted by the rowing shell.

"No, she could see how much fun it would be to be able to cook on the center island while hosting guests or making more extravagant meals with more space. And what did you buy?"

"Using that logic, I bought the patio. I can hardly wait to be out there grilling this summer. By the way, you and Gertie have an open invitation! I can picture myself out there right now! You and me, a couple of ice-cold Grain Belts, getting ready to throw the bratwurst on the grill!"

"That's the WIIFM. You both bought a kitchen remodel, but Sally bought the center island and you bought the patio. Your sales at NST aren't much different. Each decision influencer has their own WIIFM. The better you are able to help each decision influencer understand how they will get what's in it for them with your solution, the better your competitive position," explained Wally.

"Actually, that's why we chose the company for the kitchen remodel—the salesperson was thorough in discovering what each of us wanted. Here, let me add that to the list!" Steve walked into the garage and wrote *Individual Impact* on the blueprint. "Now we have ten!"

## Sales Checklist:

1) Fit
2) Trigger Event
3) Sales Target
4) Decision Making Process
5) Decision Influencers
6) Mentor
7) Trigger Priority
8) Alternatives
9) Solution Ranking
10) Individual Impact

# EPILOGUE

It was the first Saturday in August. Steve saw Wally out on his driveway with the completed rowing shell set up on a pair of slings.

"What do you think, Steve? I'm going to test it out on Lake Minnetonka today," said Wally.

"It really is beautiful, but will it row straight? Just kidding! Say, I wanted to let you know that I had my six-month review with Joe yesterday," said Steve.

"How'd it go?" asked Wally.

Steve's face lit up with a smile. "It couldn't have gone any better. We went down the list of three goals one by one.

First, Joe now feels that the sales meetings are the most enjoyable of all his internal meetings; they are focused, to the point, and based on facts, not emotions. No one is trying to defend their positioning. Everyone is pursuing opportunities the same way with no variation and without missing steps. Joe sees that we're getting one answer to his Case Study Question.

Second, the sales managers and Joe have done a wonderful job coaching. With accurate data, we make informed decisions about what to do next, or to potentially disengage. Managers coach exactly the same way. They obviously have their own management styles, but I know that they're looking at sales pursuits without variation. We've increased our win rate by 31%.

And third, even with the uptick in sales, we didn't have to hire any additional application engineers as we know exactly how to invest our resources. This has had a particularly significant impact on the sales cycles that are over twelve months. Obviously, those take the most resources. We actually freed up engineering time and that's allowed us to bring more value to our key customers—in return for more business! I can't remember the last time we were surprised by a loss. There's always visibility before the end of the customer's buying process if we are not positioned to win."

"Congratulations, Steve! I don't want to sound condescending, but I'm very proud of you."

"Thanks, Wally. I guess I've learned that sales and boatbuilding are very similar...just follow the checklist!"

"Hey, I have a present for you," said Wally with a grin as he turned into the garage. He returned to the driveway carrying a large box wrapped in a recent issue of the *St. Paul Pioneer Press*. "I'm not much for wrapping things."

Steve unwrapped the box and pulled out a large mahogany picture frame, finished exactly like the rowing shell. Mounted in the frame was the blueprint page where they had written the ten-item checklist.

"Wally, this is great! I'm going to hang it in my office! I don't know how to thank you!"

"You're quite welcome," Wally said, giving Steve a pat on the back.

"By the way, Wally, I've joined the Minnesota Boat Club! They have been rowing there since 1870. My first lesson is next Saturday morning!"

"That's wonderful, Steve! You're going to love it!"

"Would you go with me, Wally? I'd sure like the moral support! It's on Raspberry Island, just off Wabasha in St. Paul. Right on the Mississippi River."

"I think I can fit it into my schedule," Wally chuckled. "What time is the lesson?"

*Minneapolis Boathouse*

"It's at 10:00 AM. I can drive us there."

"I can be there at 10, but I have a couple of things I need to get done in the morning."

"Okay, I'll see you there, then. Thanks for going with me and for the gift!"

That Saturday, Steve pulled into the parking lot at the rowing club and saw Wally's car already there. He felt a sense of relief. He proceeded to the boathouse where the instructors were rigging the rowing shells.

Steve noticed a large crowd in one corner of the boathouse, and as he made his way over, he found Wally and Dudley in the middle of the crowd. Wally was setting up the wooden rowing shell and, well, Dudley was sitting in the rowing shell enjoying the attention.

The shell absolutely glowed in the morning sun coming through the door, the varnish showing off the beauty of the mahogany deck. Steve looked at the wooden rowing shell and then at the "plastic" shells, as Wally called them. He understood what Wally meant, and so did the crowd.

"Hey, Wally! What are you doing? Are you going to row with me?"

"No, I didn't bring a shell for me. I just brought yours."

Confused, Steve said, "What do you mean?"

"Steve, I have thoroughly enjoyed our conversations over the last six months, and I know how interested you've become in rowing, so I'd like for you to have it. Also, Gertie has her eye on a new three-seat wooden sea kayak for her, Dudley, and me, but I don't have space at the Boathouse. So, I'd like to ask you to take the rowing shell off my hands. You'll be doing me a favor. You go and show all those other rowers in their plastic and carbon fiber shells how a proper rowing shell looks and performs."

"Wally, I don't know how to thank you."

"No need to, Steve, we do stuff like this in Minnesota all the time."

"You mean Minnesooota!" Steve joked, and the two had a good laugh. "Hey, I have something for you too," Steve said. "It's not a boat or anything like that. It's fragile so don't drop it, and I'm sorry, it's not new—it's been sitting in a barrel for twenty-five years! I want to thank you for your friendship and your help."

*** 

*Six months later...*

It was a typically beautiful January day in Minnesota: − 28 degrees (but it was a dry cold), windy, and sunny.

Steve walked by the conference room outside Joe's office. The door was open, and he saw Joe, Tom, Juanita, Bob, Louie, and their new hire, Julie. He paused outside the door but didn't go in.

Steve stayed outside, eavesdropping on the conversation. They were using the checklist to review their top sales pursuits.

Louie was going through one of his pursuits. Looking at his watch, Steve realized he had a conference call in fifteen minutes, but curiosity got the best of him and he listened in.

He was pleasantly surprised when he heard Joe say, "So, Louie, tell me about this International Falls Automation pursuit. Here's a marker. Let's score it on my whiteboard."

*"Sure! I'll walk you through the checklist"*

For a moment, Steve was concerned. *What was Louie going to say?* His fear was quickly assuaged.

"Sure! Right now, they're a five. I've verified that they are a fit.

The trigger event is that they have a line of four vertical machining centers that are about twenty years old, and it's difficult to get service and parts for them. Plus, there is excessive downtime.

The sales target is four of our CDV 500 3-D printers. This is their initial step into additive machining. They plan to place a PO in thirty days.

The decision-making process is fairly complex. The vice president of manufacturing, Richard Moby, has assembled a group that includes the heads of engineering, manufacturing, and maintenance to narrow a field of three down to one. Moby has the budget available and will buy based on their recommendation—as long as it's consistent with his! So those are the decision influencers. Purchasing is involved.

My mentor says that they will try to beat us up on price, but there is consensus that our solution is the way they want to go. We may need to throw them a bone, but we can build something in for that.

Regarding trigger priority, I've been able to confirm that it's a priority for everyone. I have a question mark on alternatives because I need to confirm that Moby doesn't have any other competing projects, and for that I have a call with my mentor tomorrow.

| SALES CHECKLIST | Y/N |
|---|---|
| 1) Customer Fit | yes |
| 2) Trigger Event | yes |
| 3) Sales Target | yes |
| 4) Decision Making Process | yes |
| 5) Decision Influencers | yes |
| 6) Mentor | yes |
| 7) Trigger Priority | yes |
| 8) Alternatives | ? |
| 9) Our Solution Ranking | ? |
| 10) WIIFM | ? |
| | 70 |

I don't know about our solution ranking. The head of maintenance is very familiar with our competition. Going with us would require him to learn a new machine control and preventative maintenance procedures.

And last, I have verified the WIIFM except for the head of maintenance. Initially, I was concerned with Moby. It turns out that he has been on the job for about six months and he's looking to make his mark. When we install this new automated line, he will get recognition from the president that he is doing his job and he's the right hire. Simple. Questions?"

Joe responded, "No, that's just great, Louie. By the way, I know Richard Moby, their VP, quite well. If it would be helpful, I'd be pleased to make a call and talk with him—just let me know!

Okay, Julie, I understand you had our one-day sales checklist training and are now out in the field. Do you have a pursuit to share with us?"

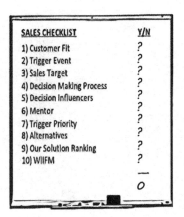

"Absolutely, it's a startup company called Damkold Manufacturing. They manufacture hydraulics for snow plows. I've had one call with them." Julie walked up to the whiteboard, erased Louie's answers, and began to write.

"So far, I don't know if they are a fit. The trigger event is that they are bringing manufacturing back into the country. But actually, that's not the trigger event, I need to find out why they are bringing it back. So, during my phone call this afternoon with Teresa, one of their manufacturing engineers, I'm going to learn more about fit, trigger event, what they are planning to buy, how they make decisions, and who is involved in making those decisions. It sounds like a lot, but it's just half a dozen questions, about ten minutes. It's simple!"

"That's pretty impressive, Julie. Your score of zero is the perfect score for this pursuit at this time. You've identified exactly what you need to do and...you're correct, it just takes a couple of minutes to use the checklist. Well done!" replied Joe.

Joe thought, *Julie has had one day of training on our checklist, and in a five-minute conversation, she covered all of the key elements our most experienced salesperson would. No variation. She coached herself. I'm confident that if the checklist ultimately shows this is not a reasonably winnable pursuit, then she will disengage before it becomes a defect and all the resources we would have invested could be better allocated.*

He now wished that his other departments ran with the precision of his sales department. *The sales team gets it right every time,* he thought. *We don't win every time, but we don't get blindsided anymore either.*

Steve walked down to his office, although he didn't feel his feet were actually touching the floor. It couldn't have gone any better!

When he was in his office, he walked over the framed checklist that Wally had made for him and slowly read each objective to himself: *Minimize variation in execution? Check! Reduce the defect rate? Check! Stop wasting resources? Check! Provide one answer? Check!*

\* \* \*

*Two years later...*

Joe had assumed the position of chairman of the board. He was not involved in the day-to-day operations of the company, but he knew everything that was going on. Joe promoted Steve to president.

Steve got into the office at around 9:15, following an early morning rowing session on the Mississippi River. The sales meeting had begun at 8:30 sharp. He walked into the conference room and took his seat, at the back of the room. The new VP of sales was running the meeting and was questioning their new hire,

Dave Oar. Dave had transferred from application engineering to sales about a month ago.

"Dave, when we discussed Precision Engineering last week, you said that the next step for you was to find out if the project was a trigger priority for all the key decision influencers. How did that go?" asked the new VP.

"It went great. I met with my mentor, and he confirmed that this is a priority for everyone. There is no reasonable doubt that they are going to make a buying decision."

"Good job, Dave. What's next?"

"I need to review our delivery time and confirm our ability to consistently hold the tolerances on their bores...but I know those aren't sales issues. From the checklist, I know the trigger event, sales target, decision-making process, and who the key decision influencers are. Basically, what I don't know is what the alternatives may be or our solution rating."

"That's great, Dave. We can talk about our ability to meet their tolerances and delivery issues after this meeting. So, during your next call, you're going to discuss alternatives and how they feel about our solution, relative to all alternatives?"

"Yep."

"That's perfect, Dave, great job."

"Lexie, can you give us an update on Super Bowl Manufacturing?"

"Sure, it's good news!"

"Wonderful! Please share it with us."

"Well, as you know, we tried to win Super Bowl Manufacturing four times. Each time it looked good. It would start out with them asking us for a quote. We would invest a ton of engineering resources and time to put together a detailed proposal. We always have thought, what an opportunity—it's such a big order! They would lead us along and make us believe that we were being considered. But when I applied the checklist on this latest opportunity, it told an entirely different story.

To begin with, they are not a fit. While there was a trigger event, I knew the sales target, and I understood the decision-making process, I wasn't able to engage all the decision influencers, and I didn't have a mentor. There was a trigger priority, but then alternatives, our solution ranking, and individual impact were all no. I was missing six of the criteria from the checklist. So, I told them that I didn't believe we were a good fit and that I was going to No Quote the project. I'd like to use those engineering resources on a net new client where I think they would be better invested. Oh, and here's the interesting part, the vice president of Super Bowl Manufacturing said he appreciated my honesty and asked that we stay involved on future projects because we're the kind of company he'd like to work with."

"Good! So, Lexie, how did it feel using the checklist and coming to the decision to walk away from this opportunity?"

"That's a great question. My knee-jerk reaction was that I lost, or

I quit. But the more I thought about it, I understood that there was nothing to lose in the first place. Now, I feel good, and the checklist really helped me change how I looked at things."

"That's fantastic, Lexie! Those are the behaviors of a top-performing salesperson."

"And Toby, can you update us about Packer Equipment?"

"I'd be happy to! I've chased these guys for three years! When I sit back and, as you suggest, nonemotionally look at the pursuit, it turns out that—I'm almost embarrassed to say—they're not a fit! There, I said it! I feel better now. I didn't get past the first item on the checklist! They don't appreciate the value we bring, and the decision influencers are not open or engaged... They just aren't a good fit. I'm firing them!"

"Great job, Toby! If they're not a fit, we can spend tremendous resources chasing them, only to lose. Toby, what you just did is execute the skills of a professional salesperson. Your time is too valuable to chase accounts like that. Now that you have additional sales time, how are you going to invest it?"

Steve settled into his chair; he could not have dreamed of a sales meeting where it was so laser focused on the key elements that a salesperson must execute in order to be successful—the checklist. The meeting demonstrated a focus on reducing variability of execution, defects, and waste.

Following the meeting, Steve asked the new VP of sales to come into his office.

Juanita walked into Steve's office, and he asked her to take a seat. "So, Juanita, how did you feel that meeting went?"

Juanita was slightly taken aback. She thought it went great, but feared that Steve had some concerns and was not satisfied.

"Well, I thought it went great," Juanita started. "We reviewed the status of ten opportunities. We identified next steps in eight of them, and we made an informed decision to disengage from two. What did you think?"

"I thought it was tremendous! Just think back to how these meetings used to go! We would talk and talk and talk and nothing of substance would be agreed upon. Next steps were often unclear, and we would never disengage from an opportunity. You're a great VP! I'd like to give you a promotion, but the next job is mine!"

"Never hurts to plan ahead!"

After work, as Steve was coming into his driveway, he saw Wally sitting in his recliner, deep in conversation with Dudley, as he often was. He paused and reflected on the time he first saw Wally and Dudley in the shop. Little did he know what their relationship would mean to him on a personal level and on a professional level. He pulled his car into his garage and walked over to the shop.

"Hey, Wally! How's it going?"

"Working away!"

"Yes, I can see that!" Steve said sarcastically. "I want to invite you and Gertie over tomorrow evening for dinner. Does that work for you?"

"I'll check with Gertie, but I know we're open."

"Great! That will be fun."

"What are we having?"

"Sally is going to make her famous tater tot hot dish!"

"Wonderful! Gertie will bring dessert. She has a new recipe for dark chocolate peanut butter bars!"

"Sounds like a plan!"

-The end-

## FOR MORE INFORMATION ON THE SALES CHECKLIST™
### VISIT WWW.THESALESCHECKLIST.INFO

- Interactive webinar for your company

- Best practices for bringing The Sales Checklist™ into your company

- Coaching The Sales Checklist™

- Support tools

- Study guides

*Author rowing mahogany shell on Mule Lake, MN*

Made in the USA
Monee, IL
07 September 2020